TREES OF AMERICA

Snow-covered trees offer an invitation to wander along country roads amid winter's beauty. The Jenne Farm, Reading, Vermont.

TREES OF AMERICA

By the Editors of OUTDOOR WORLD

Published by OUTDOOR WORLD
Country Beautiful Corporation
Waukesha, Wisconsin

ACKNOWLEDGEMENTS

The editors are grateful to the following publishers, authors and copyright holders for permission to include the following copyright material in this volume:

"Tree," by Lenore Marshall. Copyright © 1968, by Minneapolis Star and Tribune Co., Inc. Reprinted from the August 1968 issue of *Harper's* magazine by permission of the author. "Winter Trees," by William Carlos Williams, *Collected Earlier Poems.* Copyright 1938 by New Directions Publishing Corp. Reprinted by permission of New Directions Publishing Corp. Excerpts from *Day of a Stranger* by Thomas Merton. First published in the *Hudson Review.* Copyright © 1967 by The Trustees of the Merton Legacy Trust. Reprinted by permission of New Directions Publishing Corp. for the Trustees. Excerpts from *A Sand County Almanac with Other Essays on Conservation from Round River* by Aldo Leopold. Copyright © 1949, 1953, 1966 by Oxford University Press, Inc. Reprinted by permission. Peter Pauper Press, Mt. Vernon, N. Y., for permission to reprint from *Nature Thoughts.* Copyright © 1965 by Peter Pauper Press, selections by William Blake, Cicero, John Burroughs, Jonathan Edwards, Tryon Edwards, Ralph Waldo Emerson, Richard Jefferies, Charles Lamb, Walter Savage Landor, John Muir, St. Bernard de Clairvaux, Henry David Thoreau and Daniel Voorhees. Excerpts from *The Flowering Earth.* Copyright 1939 by Donald Culross Peattie. All rights reserved; G. Putnam Sons, Inc. "Are Trees as Sacred Now as They Once Were?" Copyright 1972 by St. Regis Paper Company. Excerpts from *They Knew Paul Bunyan* by E. C. Beck. Copyright 1956 by University of Michigan Press. Excerpt from *My Country and My People* by Lin Yutang. Copyright 1935, 1939 by Lin Yutang.

The editors express grateful thanks and appreciation to the following organizations and individuals for help and information as noted:

The American Forestry Association and its editor, James B. Craig, for permission to use material from *Trees Every Boy and Girl Should Know* which aided in the preparation of parts of Chapter IV, and from *Enjoying Your Trees* which aided in the preparation of parts of Chapter III — thanks are given also to the authors represented in these two American Forestry Association books, the American Forest Institute, the many Departments of Natural Resources or Environmental Resources, Historical Societies, Conservation Commissions or Chambers of Commerce of the various states or municipalities mentioned in this book that contributed resource material especially useful in the preparation of Chapters IV, V and VI; The Northeastern Forest Experiment Station, U.S.F.S., Upper Darby, Pa., for forestry research information used relating to conservation in Chapter VI; Mr. Delmar Jaquish, Assistant Regional Forester for Information and Education, Eastern Region, U.S. Forest Service, for his thoughtful appraisal of the forest ecosystem used in the introduction to Chapter VI; the U.S. Forest Service and the Information Officers of its several regions for photos, resource material and advice; the U.S. Forest Products Laboratory for its willing assistance throughout the book's preparation; the Milwaukee Public Museum for information on American Indian wood artifacts, and the American Wood Council for photos and resource material. Special thanks are given to Mr. Walter Scott of the Wisconsin Department of Natural Resources whose private book collection on trees and lifetime of knowledge in conservation and forestry aided tremendously in the preparation of this volume. Thanks also to Mrs. Kaethe Ihrig and Mr. Frederick Dobke for the generous loan of books from their personal libraries and, finally, to the many others who offered valued assistance in one way or another to make this book possible.

Pages 2-3:
Desert cottonwoods, Arizona.

Josef Muench

CONTENTS

INTRODUCTION

Trees of America is a tribute to one of this land's greatest natural resources, the only one that is renewable. Forests have figured prominently in America's history and culture from its earliest beginnings. Many great writers and poets have left us a word legacy about trees. This volume contains excerpts from the thoughtful writings of authors and naturalists such as Aldo Leopold, John Muir, Robert Frost, Henry David Thoreau, Emily Dickinson, Ralph Waldo Emerson, Gifford Pinchot, Walt Whitman, John Burroughs, Carl Sandburg and others. The book is illustrated with photographs, both full color and black and white, selected from among hundreds that depict our most beautiful trees in every season and in every part of the country.

While the continuum of the English language literary tradition reaches back to British shores (including the King James Bible), only a few of the many great English and Irish writers are quoted here, and then primarily because of a unique or particularly relevant expression. And only one or two other areas of the world are represented in these pages by words of writers from their precincts. Although this is a work about trees of America it is not an unreasoned devotion of any sort that imposes this restraint; rather, the abundance of excellent work written from intense and deep personal experience by men and women who have lived or are living in America precludes the inclusion of a vast and superb body of material by others. In fact, in the preparation of this book the editors more than once viewed keenly but wistfully the corpus of excellent writing on trees by authors in many other parts of the world.

The opening chapter, *The Seasons,* takes the reader to the Country of the Pointed Firs with Sarah Orne Jewett and then bids him to look, along with Henry David Thoreau, at bare twigs that in spring "have become a sea of verdure, and young shoots (that) have contended with one another in the race." One relives with Walt Whitman a memorable five o'clock hour on a day in early May, "the hour for strange effects in light and shade — enough to make a colorist go delirious . . . each leaf and branch of endless foliage a lit-up miracle." The reader enjoys through the eyes of Robert Frost a "hushed October morning mild," and hears from William Cullen Bryant that "winter has yet brighter scenes. . . ."

In the chapter entitled *Thoughts on Trees,* Thoreau's words speak to us clearly, piquing, with a sly challenge today as they did to his

contemporaries, "Let your walks now be a little more adventurous, ascend the hills . . . in the outskirts of our town, and probably of yours, and look over the forest, you may see — well, what I have endeavored to describe. . . . Objects are concealed from our view, not so much because they are out of the course of our visual ray as because we do not bring our minds and eyes to bear on them; for there is no power to see in the eye itself, any more than in any other jelly." It is in this chapter that Walt Whitman reminds us: "One lesson from affiliating with a tree — perhaps the greatest moral lesson anyhow from earth, rocks, animals, is that same lesson of inherency, of *what is*, without the least regard to what the looker-on (the critic) supposes or says, or whether he likes or dislikes." And it is here that William Cullen Bryant reminds us that "The groves were God's first temples."

There are over seven hundred species of trees. We hope that in the selection in *Trees Across The Land* each reader will find several that are familiar — and perhaps some unfamiliar as well — trees which will be fun to look for on the next hike in the country or while on vacation in another part of the land. This chapter includes ash, aspen, elm, hemlock, hickory, locust, maple, oak, pine, sequoia, spruce, walnut, willow and many others. There are drawings of the leaves for identification and interesting information about the trees' leaves, flowers, fruit and bark.

In *Tales and Myths* there are some fascinating true stories about trees in addition to great imaginings of ancient peoples. Readers learn from an old Indian legend why the aspen leaf trembles, how a Swedish botanist came to name the weeping willow, and how cedar is interwoven with man's history from King Solomon's temples to Northwest Coast Indian ceremonial masks. Here we find the fascinating, true, but seemingly incredible words of scholar Sir James Frazer about the King of the Wood, tall tales about that famous lumberman Paul Bunyan, and the real-life true story about Jonathan Chapman, otherwise known as Johnny Appleseed.

In *Famous Trees* the reader learns some of the fascinating history connected with many of the grand old trees of our land, such as the Evangeline Oak at Bayou Teche, St. Martinville, Louisiana, made famous when Longfellow based his poem "Evangeline" on the legend of Emmeline Labich who emigrated from Arcadia (Nova Scotia) to Maryland while her lover went to Louisiana. She was so heartbroken that she traveled to Louisiana and found her lover beneath this oak — now one of America's most famous trees. There are great trees of history such as the Washington Elm at Cambridge, the Charter Oak at Hartford, the Logan Elm near Circleville, Ohio, the Magnolia Council Tree in Charleston and the Kit Carson Pine in the Sierra Nevadas.

In the introduction to the chapter *Man and the Forest* we are reminded that the forest is an ecosystem — an ever changing natural compound of animate and inanimate components — and that it is intimately entwined with the social system of man, a relationship so sensitive that each reacts to changes in the other. Nowhere else in creation is the relationship between an ecosystem and a social system so complex, so potentially beautiful or so rewarding.

Man and the Forest takes up three important aspects of trees in their relation to man: recreation, conservation and preservation, and the uses of wood. In the recreation section Shakespeare, while applauding nature, tells us that "...this our life exempt from public haunt finds tongues in trees, books in the running brooks, sermons in stones and good in every thing." Emerson points out that "In the woods, too, a man casts off his years, as the snake his slough, and at what period soever of life, is always a child.... In the woods, we return to reason and faith." Aldo Leopold admonishes us lucidly that "The only true development in American recreational resources is the development of the perceptive faculty in Americans."

It is no accident that more and more Americans each year seek the healing balm of the beauty and stillness of the wilderness. Stillness is a precious commodity in this noisy era and to listen only to wind whistling through trees, the song of a warbler or the crackle of dead twigs as a squirrel scampers over can be a joyful experience. Man has his rhythm set in nature. His being is bound up with the sea, the sky, the trees. The rhythms of society often run counterclockwise to man's own natural rhythm. When he returns to nature he is somehow recharged. Ask a pressured young business executive what a few days' skiing on his favorite slopes will do for him, or what fishing a favorite back-country stream can mean, or hiking a forest trail. Here is the climate for quiet thought and spiritual rejuvenation, a place for re-creating body and spirit.

On the pages about the uses of wood we find that we, the public, own collectively some 136 million acres of commercial forestland or about two-thirds of an acre for every man, woman and child in the United States, and that America still has almost 75 percent as much forestland as existed here when Columbus landed. We are reminded in this section that colonial America began its existence in the forest and, while some food came from the sea or cleared land, other food for many years came directly from the forest. Forests provided pioneers with most of their basic necessities, starting often with the house itself, from its shakes or shingles at the top to its beams, joists and stringers at the bottom. Maple and cherry, walnut and butternut, poplar and chestnut and almost always pine were some of the woods associated with myriad items ranging from baskets and buckets, benches and boxes to all types of furniture. Examples of some of the handsome cedar masks carved by the Northwest Indians are included in this section as well as their beautiful totem poles.

While the products of the forest are legion perhaps none is more distinctively American than maple syrup and maple sugar. The Indians had their own method of developing maple sugar in the early 1600's, dropping hot stones in a tub of liquid and later eating the tub's contents. This was a rudimentary way to evaporate water from maple sap and while the method changed, the process is identical today.

On the conservation and preservation pages the reader is asked to think for a few moments about the demands we as a nation put upon our trees: We demand wood products of quality and in great quantity, forested recreation sites and watershed areas, natural erosion control, natural beauty of green belts around our cities, etc. This section forcefully reminds us of just how good a friend to man a tree actually is. Yearly each acre of young trees can produce enough oxygen to keep eighteen people alive! Trees aid man in so many ways — and it is easy to understand Henry Van Dyke's feelings when he wrote "He that planteth a tree is a servant of God. He provideth a kindness for many generations, and faces that he hath not seen shall bless him." In our time it is perhaps easier to understand the intensity of John Muir when he penned "It took more than 3,000 years to make some of the trees in these Western woods....Any fool can destroy trees."

I THE SEASONS

APRIL 6. — Palpable spring indeed, or the indications
of it. I am sitting in bright sunshine, at the edge of the
creek, the surface just rippled by the wind. All is solitude,
morning freshness, negligence. For companions my two king-
fishers sailing, winding, darting, dipping, sometimes capri-
ciously separate, then flying together. As noon approaches
other birds warm up. The reedy notes of the robin . . . to which
is join'd, (yes, I just hear it,) one low purr at intervals
from some impatient hylas at the pond-edge. The sibilant
murmur of a pretty stiff breeze now and then through the
trees. Then a poor little dead leaf, long frost-bound, whirls
from somewhere up aloft in one wild escaped freedom-spree
in space and sunlight, and then dashes down to the waters,
which hold it closely and soon drown it out of sight. The
bushes and trees are yet bare, but the beeches have their
wrinkled yellow leaves of last season's foliage largely left,
frequent cedars and pines yet green, and the grass not without
proofs of coming fullness. And over all a wonderfully fine
dome of clear blue, the play of light coming and going, and
great fleeces of white clouds swimming so silently.

Walt Whitman
from *Specimen Days*

May-month — month of swarming, singing, mating birds —
the bumble-bee month — month of the flowering lilac — (and
then my own birth-month.) As I jot this paragraph, I am
out just after sunrise, and down towards the creek. The
lights, perfumes, melodies — the blue birds, grass birds
and robins, in every direction — the noisy, vocal, natural
concert. For undertones, a neighboring woodpecker tapping
his tree, and the distant clarion of chanticleer. Then the
fresh-earth smells — the colors, the delicate drabs and thin
blues of the perspective. How the sun silently mounts in the
broad clear sky, on his day's journey! How the warm beams bathe
all, and come streaming kissingly and almost hot on my face.

A while since the croaking of the pond-frogs and the first
white of the dog-wood blossoms. The white cherry and pear-
blows — the wild violets, with their blue eyes looking up
and saluting my feet, as I saunter the wood-edge — the rosy
blush of budding apple-trees — a warm elasticity pervading
the air — the cedar-bushes profusely deck'd with their little
brown apples — the summer fully awakening — the convocation
of black birds, garrulous flocks of them, gathering on some
tree, and making the hour and place noisy as I sit near.

*Spring greening of young mixed Northern hardwoods overlook
the Kickapoo Valley, Wisconsin.*

Japan's famous Yoshino cherry blossoms in Washington, D. C., in full springtime bloom.

LATER. — As I write, I am seated under a big wild-cherry tree — the warm day temper'd by partial clouds and a fresh breeze, neither too heavy nor light — and here I sit long and long, envelop'd in the deep musical drone of bees, flitting, balancing, darting to and fro about me by hundreds — big fellows with light yellow jackets, great glistening swelling bodies, stumpy heads and gauzy wings — humming their perpetual rich mellow boom. (Is there not a hint in it for a musical composition, of which it should be the back-ground? some bumble-bee symphony?) How it all nourishes, lulls me, in the way most needed; the open air, the rye-fields, the apple orchards. The last two days have been faultless in sun, breeze, temperature and everything; never two more perfect days, and I have enjoy'd them wonderfully. My health is somewhat better, and my spirit at peace.

Another jotting, another perfect day: Down in the apple-trees and in a neighboring cedar were three or four russet-back'd thrushes, each singing his best, and roulading in ways I never heard surpass'd.

As I write this, two or three weeks later, I am sitting near the brook under a tulip tree, 70 feet high, thick with the fresh verdure of its young maturity — a beautiful object — every branch, every leaf perfect. From top to bottom, seeking the sweet juice in the blossoms, it swarms with myriads of these wild bees, whose loud and steady humming makes an undertone to the whole, and to my mood and the hour.

Walt Whitman
from *Specimen Days*

A bright dogwood provides a welcome to the Olympic Peninsula rain forest, Washington.

Luxuriant sparkles of dogwood blossoms brighten the haunting dark of verdant rain forest.

Overleaf: *Dogwood blossoms, Little River, Tennessee*
William A. Bake

13

A broad bay of water, a twinkling ripple to the wind-touch, and beyond, the deep black-green of the pointed firs.

Edward Simonek

Outdoor recreation, latest model.
The Maine coast — the country of the pointed firs —
a dark green campground filled with vehicles
on a point of land above shimmering azure water.

MAY 6, 5 P.M. — This is the hour for strange effects in light and shade — enough to make a colorist go delirious — long spokes of molten silver sent horizontally through the trees (now in their brightest tenderest green,) each leaf and branch of endless foliage a lit-up miracle, then lying all prone on the youthful-ripe, interminable grass, and giving the blades not only aggregate but individual splendor, in ways unknown to any other hour. I have particular spots where I get these effects in their perfection. One broad splash lies on the water, with many a rippling twinkle, offset by the rapidly deepening black-green murky-transparent shadows behind, and at intervals all along the banks. These, with great shafts of horizontal fire thrown among the trees and along the grass as the sun lowers, give effects more and more peculiar, more and more superb, unearthly, rich and dazzling.

Walt Whitman
from *Specimen Days*

JUNE 19th, 4 to 6½, P.M. — Sitting alone by the creek — solitude here, but the scene bright and vivid enough — the sun shining, and quite a fresh wind blowing (some heavy showers last night,) the grass and trees looking their best — the quiver of leaf-shadows over the paper as I write — the sky aloft, with white clouds, and the sun well declining to the west — the swift darting of many sand-swallows coming and going, their holes in a neighboring marl-bank — the odor of the cedar and oak, so palpable, as evening approaches — the old, warty, venerable oak above me — and ever, mix'd with the dual notes of the quail, the soughing of the wind through some near-by pines.

Walt Whitman
from *Specimen Days*

We were standing where there was a fine view of the harbor and its long stretches of shore all covered by the great army of the pointed firs, darkly cloaked and standing as if they waited to embark. As we looked far seaward among the outer islands, the trees seemed to march seaward still, going steadily over the heights and down to the water's edge.

Sarah Orne Jewett
from *Country of the Pointed Firs*

A crystalline dome of cloudless sky holds the silently climbing sun, the warmth bathes thick, fragrant blossoms gently brushed by a soft breeze. Rainbow shower tree, Hawaii.

Sweet is the air with the budding haws,
and the valley stretching for miles below
Is white with blossoming cherry-trees,
as if just covered with lightest snow.

Henry Wadsworth Longfellow
from "The Golden Legend"

. . . keep us here
All simply in the springing of the year.
Oh, give us pleasure in the orchard white,
Like nothing else by day, like ghosts by night.

Robert Frost
from "A Prayer in Spring"

June 1, 1854
Within a little more than a fortnight the woods, from bare
twigs, have become a sea of verdure, and young shoots have
contended with one another in the race. The leaves have
unfurled all over the country. . . .

Henry David Thoreau
from Journal

For, lo, the Winter is past, the rain is over and gone;
the flowers appear on the earth; the time of the singing of
birds is come, and the voice of the turtle is heard in our land.

Song of Solomon 2:11, 12

Nature never makes haste; her systems revolve at an even pace.
The buds swell imperceptibly, without hurry or confusion, as
though the short spring days were an eternity.

Henry David Thoreau

I am in love with this green earth.

Charles Lamb

Only that day dawns to which we are awake.

Henry David Thoreau

It is necessary to be present alone at the resurrection
of Day, in the blank silence when the sun appears. In this
completely neutral instant I receive from the Eastern woods,
the tall oaks, the one word "Day," which is never the same.

Thomas Merton
from "Day of a Stranger"

Frozen winter passes
and fickle April — one day like frosty March
and the next like budding May — gives way
to calm, warming early summer.

Summer afternoon — summer afternoon; to me those have always
been the two most beautiful words in the English language.

Henry James to Edith Wharton
from *A Backward Glance*

When all the world is young, lad,
And all the trees are green;
And every goose a swan, lad,
And every lass a queen;
Then hey for boot and horse, lad,
and round the world away:
Young blood must have its course, lad,
and every dog his day.

Charles Kingsley
from "Water Babies, Song II"

At length the summer's eternity
is ushered in by the cackle
of the flicker among the oaks
on the hill-side, and a new
dynasty begins with calm security.

Henry David Thoreau
from *Excursions*

And the wind, full of wantonness,
wooes like a lover
The young aspen-trees till they
tremble all over.

Thomas Moore
from "Lalla Rookh"

The green canopy created by tall trees
on summer afternoons provides a shimmering effect of light
and shade. Picnic Point, Madison, Wisconsin.

I thank heaven every summer's day of my life, that my lot was humbly cast within the hearing of romping brooks, and beneath the shadow of oaks. And from all the tramp and bustle of the world, into which fortune has led me in these latter years of my life, I delight to steal away for days and for weeks together, and bathe my spirit in the freedom of the old woods, and to grow young again, lying upon the brookside and counting the white clouds that sail along the sky, softly and tranquilly, even as holy memories go stealing over the vault of life.

Donald G. Mitchell

. . . as I gazed, every color seemed to deepen and glow as if the progress of the fresh sun-work were visible from hour to hour, while every tree seemed religious and conscious of the presence of God. A free man revels in a scene like this, and time goes by unmeasured.

John Muir

As imperceptibly as grief
The summer lapsed away,—
Too imperceptible, at last,
To seem like perfidy.
A quietness distilled,
As twilight long begun,
Or Nature, spending with herself
Sequestered afternoon.

Emily Dickinson

By the twenty-sixth of October the large Scarlet Oaks are in their prime, when other Oaks are usually withered. They have been kindling their fires for a week past, and now generally burst into a blaze. This alone of *our* indigenous deciduous trees (excepting the Dog-wood, of which I do not know half a dozen, and they are but large bushes) is now in its glory. The two Aspens and the Sugar-Maple come nearest to it in date, but they have lost the greater part of their leaves. Of evergreens, only the Pitch-Pine is still commonly bright.

But it requires a particular alertness, if not devotion to these phenomena, to appreciate the wide-spread, but late and unexpected glory of the Scarlet Oaks. I do not speak here of the small trees and shrubs, which are commonly observed, and which are now withered, but of the large trees. Most go in and shut their doors, thinking that bleak and colorless November has already come, when some of the most brilliant and memorable colors are not yet lit.

Henry David Thoreau
from *Excursions*

Gene Ahrens

Aspen trees — one bearing mute testimony to the affection of "J.L." for "C.L." — frame the San Juan Mountains, Pagosa Springs area, Colorado.

I like spring, but it is too young. I like summer, but it is
too proud. So I like best of all autumn, because its leaves are
a little yellow, its tone mellower, its colors richer, and it
is tinged a little with sorrow. . . . Its golden richness speaks
not of the innocence of spring, nor of the power of summer, but
of the mellowness and kindly wisdom of approaching age. It
knows the limitations of life and is content.

Lin Yutang

October is the month for painted leaves.
Their rich glow now flashes round the world.
Henry David Thoreau
from *Excursions*

Gordon Reims

Time unmeasured — every color glows, every tree seems conscious
of the presence of God. Megunticook River, Camden, Maine.

The chestnuts, lavish of their long-hid gold,
To the faint Summer, beggared now and old,
Pour back the sunshine hoarded 'neath her
favoring eye.

J. R. Lowell
from "An Indian Summer Reverie"

When Nature marks the year's decline,
Be ours to welcome it;
Pleased with the harvest hope that runs
Before the path of milder suns;
Pleased while the sylvan world displays
Its ripeness to the feeding gaze;
Pleased when the sullen winds resound the knell
Of the resplendent miracle.

William Wordsworth
from "Ode to Lycoris"

*The seasons pass — glowing reds and rusts and yellows and
browns evoke the hope and melancholy of autumn's sylvan harvest.*

All nature speaks the voice of dissolution. The highway of
history and of life is strewn with the wrecks that Time, the
great despoiler, has made. We listen sorrowfully to the autumn
winds as they sigh through dismantled forests, but we know their
breath will be soft and vernal in the spring, and the dead
flowers and withered foliage will blossom and bloom again.
And if a man dies, shall he, too, not live again?

                            Daniel Wolsey Voorhees

The damps of autumn sink into the leaves and prepare them for
the necessity of their fall; and thus insensibly are we, as years
close around us, detached from our tenacity of life by the
gentle pressure of recorded sorrow.

                            Walter Savage Landor

Wilford L. Miller

Red splotched, brindle streaked, a frost-painted apple is perfused with a beautiful blush, its straw-colored leaf silently pleading harvest time.

Apples, these I mean, unspeakably fair . . . yet not so rare but that the homeliest may have a share. Painted by the frosts, some a uniform clear bright yellow, or red, or crimson, as if their spheres had regularly revolved, and enjoyed the sun on all sides alike, —some with the faintest pink blush imaginable, —some brindled with deep red streaks like a cow, or with hundreds of fine blood-red rays running regularly from the stem-dimple to the blossom end, like meridional lines, on a straw-colored ground, —some touched with a greenish rust, like a fine lichen, here and there, with crimson blotches or eyes more or less confluent and fiery when wet, —and others gnarly, and freckled or peppered all over on the stem side with fine crimson spots on a white ground, as if accidentally sprinkled from the brush of Him who paints the autumn leaves. Others, again, are sometimes red inside, perfused with a beautiful blush, fairy food, too beautiful to eat, — apple of the Hesperides, apple of the evening sky!

Henry David Thoreau
from *Excursions*

Season of mists and mellow fruitfulness!
Close bosom friend of the maturing sun;
Conspiring with him how to load and bless
With fruit the vines that round the thatch-eaves run;
To bend with apples the moss'd cottage trees,
And fill all fruit with ripeness to the core.

John Keats
from "To Autumn"

26

OCTOBER

O hushed October morning mild,
Thy leaves have ripened to the fall;
To-morrow's wind, if it be wild,
Should waste them all.
The crows above the forest call;
To-morrow they may form and go.
O hushed October morning mild,
Begin the hours of this day slow.
Make the day seem to us less brief.
Hearts not averse to being beguiled,
Beguile us in the way you know;
Release one leaf at break of day;
At noon release another leaf;
One from our trees, one far away;
Retard the sun with gentle mist;
Enchant the land with amethyst.
Slow, slow! . . .

                                        Robert Frost

Mist rises from a small river on an early fall morning.   Tom Algire

The leaves in autumn do not change color from the blighting touch of frost, but from the process of natural decay. They fall when the fruit is ripened and their work is done. And their splendid coloring is but their graceful and beautiful surrender of life when they have finished their summer offering of service to God and man.

Tryon Edwards

Gordon Reims

The golden sugar maple — rich provider of sweet harvest — source of the Pilgrim's colonial sugar. No product of the forest is more distinctively American than maple syrup and sugar.

But winter has yet brighter scenes—he boasts
Splendours beyond what gorgeous summer knows;
Or autumn with his many fruits, and woods
All flushed with many hues.

William Cullen Bryant
from "A Winter Piece"

Announced by all the trumpets of the sky,
Arrives the snow, and, driving o'er the fields,
Seems nowhere to alight: the whited air
Hides hills and woods, the river, and the heaven.

Ralph Waldo Emerson
from "The Snow Storm"

David Sumner

Western plains bear bitter winter's desolate severity.
Cottonwoods near Morrison, Colorado, greeted a felicitous warming sun
with swelling buds but were soon covered by a capricious spring snowstorm.

In a drear-nighted December,
Too happy, happy tree,
Thy branches ne'er remember
Their green felicity.

                                        John Keats
                                        from "Stanzas"

WINTER TREES
All the complicated details
of the attiring and
the disattiring are completed!
A liquid moon
moves gently among
the long branches.
Thus having prepared their buds
against a sure winter
the wise trees
stand sleeping in the cold.

            William Carlos Williams

29

II THOUGHTS ...ON TREES

Toward midday, I gained the summit of the highest ridge in the neighborhood; and then it occurred to me that it would be a fine thing to climb one of the trees to obtain a wider outlook. But under the circumstances the choice of a tree was a serious matter. . . . After cautiously casting about, I made choice of the tallest of a group of Douglas spruces that were growing close together like a tuft of grass, no one of which seemed likely to fall unless all the rest fell with it. Though comparatively young, they were about 100 feet high, and their lithe, brushy tops were rocking and swirling in wild ecstasy. Being accustomed to climb trees in making botanical studies, I experienced no difficulty in reaching the top of this one, and never before did I enjoy so noble an exhilaration of motion. The slender tops fairly flapped and swished in the passionate torrent, bending and swirling backward and forward, round and round, tracing indescribable combinations of vertical and horizontal curves, while I clung with muscles firm braced, like a bobolink on a reed.

In its widest sweeps my tree-top described an arc of from twenty to thirty degrees, but I felt sure of its elastic temper, having seen others of the same species still more severely tried — bent almost to the ground indeed, in heavy snows — without breaking a fiber. I was therefore safe, and free to take the wind into my pulses and enjoy the excited forest from my superb outlook. The view from here must be extremely beautiful in any weather. . . .

The sounds of the storm corresponded gloriously with this wild exuberance of light and motion. The profound bass of the naked branches and boles booming like waterfalls; the quick, tense vibrations of the pine-needles, now rising to a shrill, whistling hiss, now falling to a silky murmur; the rustling of laurel groves in the dells, and the keen metallic click of leaf on leaf — all this was heard in easy analysis when the attention was calmly bent. . . .

I kept my lofty perch for hours, frequently closing my eyes to enjoy the music by itself, or to feast quietly on the delicious fragrance that was streaming past. The fragrance of the woods was less marked than that produced during warm rain, when so many balsamic buds and leaves are steeped like tea; but, from the chafing of resiny branches against each other, and the incessant attrition of myriads of needles, the gale was spiced to a very tonic degree. And besides the fragrance from these local sources there were traces of scents brought from afar. . . .

Winds are advertisements of all they touch, however much or little we may be able to read

A pervasive sense of peace far from the madding crowd.

them; telling their wanderings even by their scents alone. . . .

And when we look around over an agitated forest, we may see something of the wind that stirs it, by its effects upon the trees. Yonder it descends in a rush of waterlike ripples, and sweeps over the bending pines from hill to hill. Nearer, we see detached plumes and leaves, now speeding by on level currents, now whirling in eddies, or, escaping over the edges of the whirls, soaring aloft on grand, upswelling domes of air, or tossing on flamelike crests. Smooth, deep currents, cascades, falls, and swirling eddies, sing around every tree and leaf, and over all the varied topography of the region with telling changes of form, like mountain rivers conforming to the features of their channels.

We all travel the milky way together, trees and men; but it never occurred to me until this storm-day, while swinging in the wind, that trees are travelers, in the ordinary sense. They make many journeys, not extensive ones, it is true; but our own little journeys, away and back again, are only little more than tree-wavings — many of them not so much.

When the storm began to abate, I dismounted and sauntered down through the calming woods. The storm-tones died away, and, turning toward the east, I beheld the countless hosts of the forests hushed and tranquil, towering above one another on the slopes of the hills like a devout audience. The setting sun filled them with amber light, and seemed to say, while they listened, "My peace I give unto you."

As I gazed on the impressive scene, all the so-called ruin of the storm was forgotten, and never before did these noble woods appear so fresh, so joyous, so immortal.

John Muir
from *The Mountains of California*

S. J. Krasemann

Happy memories of youth pass in garlands through one's soul at the witness of each day's renewal. The fresh earth fragrance suffuses the soft meadow mist and the sun hazes upward beyond a grove of hickory.

Dormant boughs of elms awaken in the flooding radiance of a warming spring sun on a Wisconsin farm.

S. J. Krasemann

A light exists in spring
    Not present on the year
At any other period.
    When March is scarcely here

A color stands abroad
    On solitary hills
That science cannot overtake,
    But human nature *feels*.

It waits upon the lawn;
    It shows the furthest tree
Upon the furthest slope we know;
    It almost speaks to me.

Then, as horizons step,
    Or noons report away,
Without the formula of sound,
    It passes, and we stay:

A quality of loss
    Affecting our content,
As trade had suddenly encroached
    Upon a sacrament.

Emily Dickinson
"A Light Exists in Spring"

Judy Manna

Two roads diverged in a yellow wood,
And sorry I could not travel both
And be one traveler, long I stood
And looked down one as far as I could
To where it bent in the undergrowth;

Then took the other, as just as fair,
And having perhaps the better claim,
Because it was grassy and wanted wear;
Though as for that the passing there
Had worn them really about the same,

And both that morning equally lay
In leaves no step had trodden black.
Oh, I kept the first for another day!
Yet knowing how way leads on to way,
I doubted if I should ever come back.

I shall be telling this with a sigh
Somewhere ages and ages hence:
Two roads diverged in a wood, and I —
I took the one less traveled by,
and that has made all the difference.

Robert Frost
"The Road Not Taken"

The spruce, the hemlock, and the pine will not countenance
despair. . . . The doctrines of despair, of spiritual or political
tyranny or servitude, were never taught by such as shared the
serenity of nature. . . . They are sick and diseased imaginations
who would toll the world's knell so soon.

Henry David Thoreau
from *Excursions*

One lesson from affiliating a tree — perhaps the greatest
moral lesson anyhow from earth, rocks, animals, is that same
lesson of inherency, of *what is*, without the least regard
to what the looker-on (the critic) supposes or says, or whether
he likes or dislikes. What worse — what more general malady
pervades each and all of us, our literature, education,
attitude toward each other, (even toward ourselves,) than a
morbid trouble about *seems*, (generally temporarily seems
too,) and no trouble at all, or hardly any, about the sane,
slow-growing, perennial, real parts of character, books,
friendship, marriage — humanity's invisible
foundation and hold-together?

Walt Whitman
from *Specimen Days*

*Walking into a Vermont autumn on a country road
flanked by maples near South Corinth.*

Stalwart white pine and hardwood silhouetted in the early morning sun.

Believe one who knows: you will find something greater in woods
than in books. Trees and stones will teach you that which you
can never learn from masters.

St. Bernard

Peace and quiet under the snow-lined elms of
a New England village, Warren, Maine.

Gordon Reims

But it sometimes happens that I cannot easily shake off the
village. The thought of some work will run in my head, and I am
not where my body is, — I am out of my senses. In my walks I
would fain return to my senses. What business have I in the woods,
if I am thinking of something out of the woods? I suspect myself.

Henry David Thoreau
from *Excursions*

Surely there is something in the unruffled calm of nature
that overawes our little anxieties and doubts: the sight of the
deep-blue sky, and the clustering stars above, seem to impart a
quiet to the mind.

Jonathan Edwards
from "Thoughts on Trees"

Up! up! my Friend, and quit your books;
Or surely you'll grow double;
Up! up! my Friend, and clear your looks;
Why all this toil and trouble?

. . . Come forth into the light of things
Let Nature be your teacher. . . .

One impulse from a vernal wood
May teach you more of man,
Of moral evil and of good,
than all the sages can.

. . . Enough of Science and of Art;
Close up those barren leaves;
Come forth, and bring with you a heart
That watches and receives.

William Wordsworth
from "The Tables Turned"

Walking into an ancient forest a man becomes displaced in time.

Every tree like every man must decide for itself — will it
live in the alluring forest and struggle to the top where alone is
sunlight or give up the fight and content itself with the shade —
or leave this delectable land of loam and water and be satisfied
with the waste and barren plains that are not desirable.

Ernest Thompson Seton
from *Foresters' Manual*

Why should we be in such haste to succeed and in such
desperate enterprises? If a man does not keep pace with his
companions, perhaps it is because he hears a different drummer.
Let him step to the music which he hears,
however measured or far away.

Henry David Thoreau
from *Walden*

*'Tis a wonderfully agreeable occupation, to lie on one's
back in the forest and stare upward. It seems that the maple
does not rise out of the earth, but hangs suspended.*

W. J. Wiekie

In the sequestered primeval forest
a humble paean to God rises
from the deep of man's soul.

The most cheerful thing I know is the calm, the silence,
which are so delicious, both in the forest and the fields. For
me it is true humanity and great poetry.

Jean Francois Millet
from *Jean Francois Millet: His Life and Letters*

The groves were God's first temples.
Ere man learned
To hew the shaft, and lay the architrave,
And spread the roof above them — ere he framed
The lofty vault, to gather and roll back
The sound of anthems; in the darkling wood,
Amidst the cool and silence, he knelt down,
And offered to the Mightiest solemn thanks
And supplication. For his simple heart
Might not resist the sacred influences
Which, from the stilly twilight of the place,
And from the gray old trunks that high in heaven
Mingled their mossy boughs, and from the sound
Of the invisible breath that swayed at once
All their green tops, stole over him, and bowed
His spirit with the thought of boundless power
And inaccessible majesty. . . .

William Cullen Bryant
from "A Forest Hymn"

In all great arts as in trees it is the height that charms us;
we care nothing for the roots, or trunks, yet it could not be
without the aid of these.

Marcus Tullius Cicero

Wildwood privacy in the misty, soft dusk of a springtime noon.
Mountain hemlock and phacelia flowers in the Great Smoky Mountains.

I am in awe of this small seed,
Its perfect design and the design within:
The great sequoia tree sleeping, waiting
To send down its first root
No bigger than an eyelash.
The parent tree stands near,
Its fluted bark defying malady and fire,
Its body embracing a river of sap
Flowing upward to a pollen-yellowed crown
Known only to flying things, to sun and storm.
Here, far below, roots graze through acres
Of true, sustaining earth.
While ages were rising and blooming and dying,
While man was going his tender, learning, savage
And fragile way,
This tree was growing —
In snows of the unnamed Sierra Nevadas
And ancient, nameless Pacific winds,
Aloof in this dusky grove,
Its life begun two thousand years
Before Christ was born.

Sanora Babb

That Sequoia can grow and is growing on as dry ground as any of its neighbors or rivals, we have seen proved over and over again. "Why, then," it will be asked, "are the Big Tree groves always found on well-watered spots?" Simply because Big Trees give rise to streams. It is a mistake to suppose that the water is the cause of the groves being there. On the contrary, the groves are the cause of the water being there. The roots of this immense tree fill the ground, forming a sponge which hoards the bounty of the clouds and sends it forth in clear perennial streams instead of allowing it to rush headlong in short-lived destructive floods. Evaporation is also checked, and the air kept still in the shady sequoia depths, while thirsty robber winds are shut out.

Since, then, it appears that Sequoia can and does grow on as dry ground as its neighbors and that the greater moisture found with it is an effect rather than a cause of its presence, the notions as to the former greater extension of the species and its near approach to extinction, based on its supposed dependence on greater moisture, are seen to be erroneous. Indeed, all my observations go to show that in case of prolonged drought the sugar pines and firs would die before Sequoia. Again, if the restricted and irregular distribution of the species be interpreted as the result of the desiccation of the range, then, instead of increasing in individuals toward the south, where the rainfall is less, it should diminish.

John Muir
from "The Sequoia"

The conifers illustrate better than others of our trees the process and plan of growth. Thus a seedling pine has a tassel or two at the top of a slender shoot, next year it has a second shoot and a whorl corresponding exactly with its vigor that season, until the tree is so tall that the lower whorls die, and their knots are overlaid by fresh layers of timber. The timber grows smoothly over them, but they are there just the same, and anyone carefully splitting open one of these old forest patriarchs, can count on the spinal column the years of its growth, and learn in a measure how it fared each season.

Ernest Thompson Seton
from *Foresters' Manual*

JUNE 23, 1852

There are interesting groves of young soft white pines eighteen feet high, whose vigorous yellowish-green shoots of this season, from three to eighteen inches long, at the extremities of all the branches, contrast remarkably with the dark green of the old leaves. I observe that these shoots are bent, and, what is more remarkable, all one way, *i.e.*, to the east, almost at a right angle the topmost ones, and I am reminded of the observation in Henry's Adventures, that the Indians guided themselves in cloudy weather by this mark. All these shoots, excepting those low down on the east side, are bent toward the east. I am very much pleased with this observation, confirming that of the Indians. I was singularly impressed when I first observed that all the young pines in this pasture obeyed this law, without regard to the direction of the wind or the shelter of other trees. To make myself more sure of the direction, as it was not easy to determine it exactly, standing on one side, where so many shoots were bent in the air, I went behind the trees on the west till the bent shoot appeared as a straight line, and then, by observing my shadow and guessing at the time of day, I decided that their direction was due east. This gives me more satisfaction than any observation which I have made for a long time. . . . How few civilized men probably have ever made this observation, so important to the savage!

JUNE 24

I am disappointed to notice to-day that most of the pine-tops incline to the west, as if the wind had to do with it.

Henry David Thoreau
"Pine Shoots"
from Journal

What profusion is there in His work! When trees
blossom there is not a single breastpin, but a whole bosom-full
of gems; and of leaves that have so many suits that they can
throw them away to the winds all summer long. What unnumbered
cathedrals has He geared in the forest shades, vast and grand,
full of curious carvings, and haunted evermore
by tremulous music. . . .

Henry Ward Beecher
from *Life Thoughts*

The tree which moves some to tears of joy is in the eyes
of others only a green thing which stands in the way. Some see
Nature all ridicule and deformity, and by these I shall not
regulate my proportions; and some scarce see Nature at all. But
to the eyes of the man of imagination, Nature is Imagination
itself. As a man is, so he sees.

William Blake

OCT. 9, 1857
It has come to this — that the lover of art is one, and the lover
of nature another, though true art is but the expression of our
love of nature. It is monstrous when one cares but little about
trees and much about Corinthian columns, and yet this is
exceedingly common.

Henry David Thoreau
from Journal

Let your walks now be a little more adventurous; ascend the
hills. If, about the last of October, you ascend any hill in the
outskirts of our town, and probably of yours, and look over the
forest, you may see — well, what I have endeavored to describe.
All this you surely *will* see, and much more, if you are
prepared to see it, — if you *look* for it. Otherwise, regular
and universal as this phenomenon is, whether you stand on the
hill-top or in the hollow, you will think for threescore years
and ten that all the wood is, at this season, sere and brown.
Objects are concealed from our view, not so much because they
are out of the course of our visual ray as because we do not
bring our minds and eyes to bear on them; for there is no power

to see in the eye itself, any more than in any other jelly. We
do not realize how far and widely, or how near and narrowly, we
are to look. The greater part of the phenomena of Nature are for
this reason concealed from us all our lives. Nature does not
cast pearls before swine. There is just as much beauty visible to
us in the landscape as we are prepared to appreciate, — not a
grain more. . . . A man sees only what concerns him.

Henry David Thoreau
from *Excursions*

The existence of trees was a prerequisite of conceptual
thought. . . . It was under the auspices of these ancient boughs
that he [man] appeared. And having appeared he was destined to
interfere with the Order of Nature. The very forests were doomed.

Donald Culross Peattie

. . . these shades
Are still the abodes of gladness; the thick roof
Of green and stirring branches is alive
And musical with birds, that sing and sport
In wantonness of spirit; while below
The squirrel, with raised paws and form erect,
Chirps merrily. Throngs of insects in the shade
Try their thin wings and dance in the warm beam
That waked them into life. Even the green trees
Partake the deep contentment; as they bend
To the soft winds, the sun from the blue sky
Looks in and sheds a blessing on the scene.
Scarce less the cleft-born wild-flower seems to enjoy
Existence, than the winged plunderer
That sucks its sweets. The mossy rocks themselves,
And the old and ponderous trunks of prostrate trees
That lead from knoll to knoll a causey rude,
Or bridge the sunken brook, and their dark roots,
With all their earth upon them, twisting high,
Breathe fixed tranquillity. The rivulet
Sends forth glad sounds, and tripping o'er its bed
Of pebbly sands, or leaping down the rocks,
Seems, with continuous laughter, to rejoice
In its own being.

William Cullen Bryant
from *The Entrance to a Wood*

Ed Cooper

Pine trees at Tenaya Lake in the Sierra Nevada Mountains of California.

There is a pleasure in the pathless woods,
There is a rapture on the lonely shore,
There is a society, where none intrudes,
By the deep Sea, and music in its roar:
I love not Man the less, but Nature more,
From these our interviews, in which I steal
From all I may be, or have been before,
To mingle with the Universe, and feel
What I can ne'er express, yet cannot all
conceal.

Lord Byron

I fall in with persons, now and then, who profess to care
nothing for a path when walking in the woods. They do not choose
to travel in other people's footsteps, . . . but count it their
mission to lay out a new road every time they go afield. . . . It
is well enough to strike into the trackless forest once in a while;

to wander you know not whither, . . . to lie down in a strange
place, and for an hour imagine yourself the explorer of a new
continent: but if the mind be awake (as, alas, too often it is not),
you may walk where you will, in never so well known a corner,
and you will see new things, and think new thoughts, and return to
your house, a new man.

Bradford Torrey
from *American Fields and Forests*

I had withdrawn in forest, and my song
Was swallowed up in leaves that blew alway;
And to the forest edge you came one day
(This was my dream) and looked and pondered long,
But did not enter, though the wish was strong:
You shook your pensive head as who should say,
'I dare not — too far in his footsteps stray —
He must seek me would he undo the wrong.'

Not far, but near, I stood and saw it all
Behind low boughs the trees let down outside;
And the sweet pang it cost me not to call
And tell you that I saw does still abide.
But 'tis not true that thus I dwelt aloof,
For the wood wakes, and you are here for proof.

Robert Frost
from "A Dream Pang"

I went to the woods because I wished to live deliberately,
to front only the essential facts of life, and see if I could
not learn what it had to teach, and not, when I came to die,
discover that I had not lived.

Henry David Thoreau
from *Walden*

Who has seen the wind?
Neither I nor you:
But when the leaves hang trembling
The wind is passing thro'.

Who has seen the wind?
Neither you nor I:
But when the trees bow down their heads
The wind is passing by.

Christina G. Rossetti
"Who Has Seen the Wind?"

Loveliest of trees, the cherry now
Is hung with bloom along the bough. . . .

A. E. Housman
from "Loveliest of Trees"
from *A Shropshire Lad*

If tired of trees I seek again mankind,
    Well I know where to hie me — in the dawn,
    To a slope where the cattle keep the lawn.
There amid lolling juniper reclined,
Myself unseen, I see in white defined
    Far off the homes of men, and farther still,
    The graves of men on an opposing hill,
Living or dead, whichever are to mind.

And if by noon I have too much of these
    I have but to turn on my arm, and lo,
    The sun-burned hillside sets my face aglow,
My breathing shakes the bluet like a breeze,
    I smell the earth, I smell the bruisèd plant,
    I look into the crater of the ant.

Robert Frost
from "The Vantage Point"

Perchance, in the afternoon of such a day, when the water
is perfectly calm and full of reflections, I paddle gently down the
main stream, and, turning up the Assabet, reach a quiet cove, where
I unexpectedly find myself surrounded by myriads of leaves, like
fellow-voyagers, which seem to have the same purpose, or want of
purpose, with myself. See this great fleet of scattered leaf-boats
which we paddle amid, in this smooth river-bay, each one curled up
on every side by the sun's skill, each nerve a stiff spruce-knee —
like boats of hide, and of all patterns, Charon's boat probably
among the rest, and some with lofty prows and poops, like the
stately vessels of the ancients, scarcely moving in the sluggish
current — like the great fleets, the dense Chinese cities of
boats, with which you mingle on entering some great mart, some
New York or Canton, which we are all steadily approaching together.
How gently each has been deposited on the water! No violence has
been used towards them yet, though, perchance,
palpitating hearts were present at the launching.

Henry David Thoreau
from *Excursions*

A sugaring house is hidden in the midst of a Vermont sugar bush.

III TALES AND MYTHS

Gus Wolfe

Lights and shades and rare effects on tree-foliage — transparent greens, grays, etc., all in sunset pomp and dazzle. The clear beams are now on the quilted, seam'd, bronze-drab, lower tree-trunks, shadow'd except at this hour — now flooding their old columnar ruggedness with strong light, unfolding silent, shaggy charm, the solid bark, the expression of harmless impassiveness, with many a bulge and gnarl unreck'd before. In the revealings of such light, such exceptional hour, such mood, one does not wonder at the old story fables of people seiz'd extatic with the mystic realism of the resistless silent strength in them — *strength,* which after all is perhaps the last, completest, highest beauty.

Walt Whitman
from *Specimen Days*

50

The gnarled, mystic reality of ancient and resistless strength has stimulated creation of fantastic fables.

Who does not know Turner's picture of the Golden Bough? The scene, suffused with the golden glow of imagination in which the divine mind of Turner steeped and transfigured even the fairest natural landscape, is a dreamlike vision of the little woodland lake of Nemi — "Diana's Mirror," as it was called by the ancients. No one who has seen that calm water, lapped in a green hollow of the Alban hills, can ever forget it. The two charactertistic Italian villages which slumber on its banks, and the equally Italian palace whose terraced gardens descend steeply to the lake, hardly break the stillness and even the solitariness of the scene. Diana herself might still linger by this lonely shore, still haunt these woodlands wild. . . .

. . . According to one story the worship of Diana at Nemi was instituted by Orestes, who, after killing Thoas, King of the Tauric Chersonese (the Crimea), fled with his sister to Italy, bringing with him the image of the Tauric Diana hidden in a faggot of sticks. After his death his bones were transported from Africa to Rome and buried in front of the temple of Saturn, on the Capitoline slope, beside the temple of Concord. The bloody ritual which legend ascribed to the Tauric Diana is familiar to classical readers; it is said that every stranger who landed on the shore was sacrificed on her altar. But transported to Italy, the rite assumed a milder form. Within the sanctuary at Nemi grew a certain tree of which no branch might be broken. Only a runaway slave was allowed to break off, if he could, one of its boughs. Success in the attempt entitled him to fight the priest in single combat, and if he slew him he reigned in his stead with the title of King of the Wood (*Rex Nemorensis*). According to the public opinion of the ancients the fateful branch was the Golden Bough which, at the Sibyl's bidding, Aeneas plucked before he essayed the perilous journey to the world of the dead. The flight of the slave represented, it was said, the flight of Orestes; his combat with the priest was a reminiscence of the human sacrifices once offered to the Tauric Diana. This rule of succession by the sword was observed down to imperial times; for amongst his other freaks Caligula, thinking that the priest of Nemi had held office too long, hired a more stalwart ruffian to slay him; and a Greek traveller, who visited Italy in the age of the Antonines, remarks that down to his time the priesthood was still the prize of victory in a single combat.

Sir James G. Frazer
from *The Golden Bough*

Cedars and Aspens

Riding through the forests of Morocco, Marshal Lylutey, who had defeated the Moroccan forces, came upon giant cedars that had been smashed and torn in a violent storm, according to author Andre Maurois. The marshal commanded his aide, "Plant new cedars here." The aide broke out in laughter and told Lylutey that it took two thousand years to grow cedars like the ones destroyed in the storm. The marshal quickly replied, "Two thousand years? Then we must begin at once!"

The cedar is interwoven with much of man's history. King Solomon's temple, so legend has it, was built of cedar, as were many Egyptian mummy cases. Egyptian solar boats unearthed in the 1950's near the pyramid of Giza were made of Lebanese cedar roughly twenty-eight centuries ago. The sacred Hebrew Ark of the Covenant probably was made of the wood.

Approximately four hundred ancient trees tenaciously clinging to a rocky bowl carved high in mountains on Lebanon's Mediterranean coast comprise the true and historic "cedars of Lebanon." The grove has one-hundred-foot giants that, according to legend, developed and grew from cedar rods pressed into the ground by Christ and his disciples. A second legend claims that God himself planted the trees and the Bible appears to confirm this when it says in Psalms, 104:16,17, "The trees of the Lord are full of sap; the cedars of Lebanon, which he hath planted; where the birds make their nests: as for the stork, the fir trees are her house."

Symbols of Goodness, Longevity, Power and Prosperity, the lofty cedars of Lebanon are referred to over thirty times in the Bible.

Our Northwest Indians hollowed out their war canoes from cedar, carved totem poles of it (see Chapter VI), even used it to make ropes and fish lines, blankets and clothing from its bark.

Its extremely narrow grain makes cedar good for pencils (they sharpen better). This narrow grain is due to the fact that there is little difference between the tree's spring and summer growth.

Like the cedar, some other trees have played important parts in history, while still others have become well known because of myths and legends surrounding them, and a few other species are famous because they were the personal favorites of great men. These stories make fascinating reading, from the myths of the evergreens to the tale of the Washington Elm (see Chapter IV) to the exciting drama of the colorful American clipper ships with their white pine masts.

U. S. Forest Service

Strength, massive and enduring, is perhaps the ultimate beauty.

The aspen helped to write the unsung history of our early West. Scores of explorers, mountain men and *coureurs de bois* such as Jim Bridger, Kit Carson, Bonneville, Ashley and others sought out the aspen first in order to trap beaver. The latter, literally *woods runners,* were French or French-Indian half-breeds who ranged with courage far and wide through the Western wilderness. Legend has it that these *coureurs* would not enter a cabin made of aspen logs since it was the supposed wood selected for the Cross, as evidenced by the quaking leaves that never ceased to tremble from that awful date.

Among the many Indian legends about trees there is one that says the Great Spirit visited the earth one year and a naive and guileless aspen was too wild to fear and too innocent to bow. The Great Spirit misunderstood and decreed a "forever tremble" onto the little tree. Modern man is not so far from the savage heart in the melancholy pause of Indian Summer, when the seasonal farewell is everywhere. It is only natural to reach for deathless legends to keep the vision alive. Not long after Indian Summer is gone night winds will bare the leafy branches, and soon all will be quiet under the white cloth of winter.

A recent news release probably had many children across the land shouting "I knew it!"

(continued on p. 56)

Dazzling golden aspen in pure Western mountain air,
a rare effect of light and shadow.

54

The aspen served as a practical guide to beaver for fur-seeking mountain men of the 1830's and 1840's; earlier it was the subject of Indian tree legends.

55

What child, looking at aspen leaves in the fall sunshine, has not known in his heart that they were *really* golden? U.S. Geological Survey scientists indicated a gold prospecting technique now is being used in the Empire Mining District of Clear Creek County, Colorado, that is based upon aspen leaves and pine needles. Geochemical tests were made of the humus-rich forest soil. These tests showed that gold absorbed through tree roots was deposited in the leaf and needle litter on the ground. The litter decays and the mull layer of the soil apparently becomes very slightly enriched with gold.

Johnny Appleseed

Johnny Appleseed was very much a real person who became a legend in his own time. This was the nickname given to one Jonathan Chapman (1774-1845), American orchardist and folk hero. Born in Massachusetts, he wandered westward to Pennsylvania, Ohio, Illinois and Indiana, leading a nomadic life for fifty years, preaching and distributing apple seeds to everyone he met. It has been said that the orchards of these four states owe their origin to Johnny Appleseed.

Harper's magazine, dated November 1871, carried an authentic and fascinating article about this pioneer hero, excerpted below. This article has been the basis for most, if not all, of the writing that has been done since about the real-life exploits of Johnny Appleseed:

"In personal appearance (he) was a small, wiry man, full of restless activity, he had long, dark hair, a scanty beard that was never shaved, and keen black eyes that sparkled with a peculiar brightness. His dress was of the oddest description. Generally, even in the coldest weather, he went barefooted, but sometimes, for his long journeys, he would make himself a rude pair of sandals; at other times he would wear any cast-off foot-covering he chanced to find — a boot on one foot and an old brogan or moccasin on the other. It appears to have been a matter of conscience with him never to purchase shoes, although he was rarely without money enough to do so. . . . His dress was generally composed of cast-off clothing, that he had taken in payment for apple-trees . . . . In his later years, however, he seems to have thought that even his kind of second-hand raiment was too luxurious, as his principal garment was made of a coffee sack, in which he cut holes for his head and arms to pass through, and pronounced it a 'very serviceable cloak, and as good clothing as any man need wear.' In the matter of headgear his taste was equally unique; his first experiment was with a tin vessel that served to cook his mush, but this was open to the objection that

it did not protect his eyes from the beams of the sun; so he constructed a hat of pasteboard with an immense peak in front, and having thus secured an article that combined usefulness with economy, it became his permanent fashion."

The *Harper's* article states that ". . . the first reliable trace of our modest hero finds him in the Territory of Ohio in 1801, with a horse-load of apple seeds, which he planted in various places on and about the borders of Licking Creek, the first orchard thus originated by him being on the farm of Isaac Stadden, in what is now known as Licking County, in the State of Ohio. During the five succeeding years, although he was undoubt-

Gene Ahrens

The apple tree has produced fables and legends in the growth of our nation, one of the more fantastic being true — that of Jonathan Chapman, known as Johnny Appleseed.

edly following the same strange occupation, we have no authentic account of his movements until we reach a pleasant spring day in 1806, when a pioneer settler in Jefferson County, Ohio, noticed a peculiar craft, with a remarkable occupant and a curious cargo, slowly dropping down with the current of the Ohio River. It was 'Johnny Appleseed' by which name Jonathan Chapman was afterward known in every log-cabin from the Ohio River to the Northern Lakes, and westward to the prairies of what is now the State of Indiana.

This oddly shaped Southwest desert tree, the Joshua, named by Mormon pioneers who saw in it a likeness to the biblical figure with arms outstretched toward heaven, belongs to the lily family but has adapted itself to arid or semiarid regions.

"With two canoes lashed together he was transporting a load of apple seeds to the Western frontier, for the purpose of creating orchards on the farthest verge of white settlements. A long and tiresome voyage it was, as a glance at the map will show, and must have occupied a great deal of time, as the lonely traveler stopped at every inviting spot to plant the seeds and make his infant nurseries. Whether impelled in his eccentricities by some absolute misery of the heart which could only find relief in incessant motion, or governed by a benevolent monomania, his whole after-life was devoted to the work of planting apple seeds in remote places. The seeds he gathered from the cider-presses of western Pennsylvania; but this canoe voyage in 1806 appears to have been the only occasion upon which he adopted that method of transporting them, as all subsequent journeys were made on foot. Having planted his stock of seeds, he would return to Pennsylvania for a fresh supply.

"In the summer of 1847, when his labors had literally borne fruit over a hundred thousand square miles of territory, at the close of a warm day, after traveling twenty miles, he entered the house of a settler in Allen County, Indiana, and was, as usual, warmly welcomed. He declined to eat with the family, but accepted some bread and milk, which he partook of sitting on the door-step and gazing on the setting sun. Later in the evening he delivered his 'news right fresh from heaven' by reading the Beatitudes. Declining other accom-

A tough, hardy lumberman and a massive white pine — both the sort that make wonderful folk-heroes.

Symbolic Patriotic Trees

Trees seem to have been associated with patriotism, as well as religion, particularly when in recent centuries nations have thrown off oppression. A "tree of liberty" is a post or actual tree set up by the people, hung with flags and devices and crowned with a "cap of liberty" (a cap hoisted or elevated in some way, usually made of red felt).

In the United States, poplars and other trees (see Chapter IV) were planted during the War of Independence as growing symbols of freedom. The revolutionary Jacobins in Paris planted trees of liberty in 1790, and decorated each with tri-colored ribbons, circles to indicate unity, triangles to signify equality and a cap of liberty *(bonnet rouge)*. Trees of liberty were also planted by the Italians during their revolution of 1848.

Paul Bunyan

It was among the toilers of the forests that the legends of Paul Bunyan originated — Paul Bunyan, the greatest lumberjack who ever skidded a log, who with the aid of his wonderful blue ox and his crew of hardy lumbermen cleared one hundred million board feet of pine from a single forty and performed other wondrous feats.

Wherever there is semipermanent isolation from the outside world of large groups of people engaged in the same occupation or at least having a community of interests, there is almost certain to spring up in time tales peculiar to that community. Such legends existed among the Great North lumbermen.

Whether a flesh-and-blood lumberjack named Paul Bunyan ever lived was never determined by scholarly researchers when they interviewed, in the early days of this century, the durable survivors of the lusty timber-crashing 1880's and 90's. They did find older men who claimed to have known Paul, who even pointed out the supposed location of his grave in northern Minnesota. One half-breed lumberman asserted positively that there *was* a Paul Bunyan and that the place where he cut his hundred million feet from a single forty was actually on the map. They also found characters still living about whose prowess as lumbermen exaggerated stories were already being told. Some of those tales continued to be told — and enlarged upon — after their real–life heroes had died. Paul Bunyan probably came into existence in like manner.

. . . and the Paul Bunyan trees were even larger than this — he cut a million board feet from a single forty! The Founder's Tree, Sequoia sempervirens.

modation, he slept as usual, on the floor, and in the early morning he was found with his features all aglow with a supernal light, and his body so near death that his tongue refused its office. The physician, who was hastily summoned, pronounced him dying, but added that he had never seen a man in so placid a state at the approach of death. At seventy-two years of age, forty-six of which had been devoted to his self-imposed mission, he ripened into death as naturally and beautifully as the seeds of his own planting had grown into fiber and bud and blossom and the matured fruit.''

Supplies for the lumber camps were brought by water in boats whenever possible. The water routes were often impeded by rapids, no great problem for small boats which could be dragged or portaged by lumberjacks. But for the larger boats the problem was tougher. Cables were attached to the boats, running to a windlass above the rapids. A score or more of lumberjacks would strain at the windlass handles to slowly inch the boat upstream. After a stretch of this rugged labor they would stay the capstan by inserting a pawl (a pivoted tongue or sliding bolt on one part of a machine, adapted to fall into notches on another part, so as to prevent backward motion) into the gear. It held — and it was said that the little pawl had the strength of fifty lumberjacks. Thus Little Pawl became the jack's symbol for tough strength. Profound respect was tendered to anyone about whom it could be said, "He is as strong as Little Pawl."

The jacks sat around the fire at night and amused themselves by spinning yarns. Little Paul became the hero of many of these tales. As the lumbermen moved from camp to camp they would tell stories of some mighty Paul they had known in another camp. The exploits of the mighty Pauls gained always in the retelling. The lumberjack trade had many fancy liars.

The stories of Paul surely started in the camps of Wisconsin and Michigan and Paul developed rapidly from a sobriquet for any powerful lumberjack to a single, mighty, legendary character. As the stories grew, the legend took shape. Paul became a definite character, not just a lumberjack, but a boss; not just a boss, he had his own camp; and his camp had jacks just a notch or two down the tree from the mighty Paul.

For forty years the legend of Paul lived and grew and finally, in the 90's, Paul got a surname. He was given the French name, Bunyon, after the French Canadian Paul Bunyon — a real man who lived and breathed and then became a legend.

So there really *was* a Paul Bunyon, a Paul Bunyon who was a strapping farmer, not a lumberjack, and he was famous as a soldier. He was the French hero of the Papineau rebellion of 1837, when the French Canadians revolted against the British Government. A bearded giant, he performed great feats on the battlefield. This raging Samsonlike soldier was much admired by the French Canadians. They told and retold stories of his great bravery in battle and of his physical prowess. These stories of him became a legend.

When the French Canadians left their homeland to become lumberjacks in the lake states they carried the mighty tales of Paul Bunyon with them to the woods. There the two characters were merged as the tales were told over and over, and so Paul, the lumberjack, acquired the surname, Bunyan. By then the eighteenth century was nearly done and the character of Paul Bunyan was complete, right down to a complete name.

He was a powerful giant, seven feet tall (originally) and with a stride of seven feet. He was famous throughout the lumbering districts for his physical strength and for the ingenuity with which he met difficult situations. He was so powerful that no man could successfully oppose him, and his ability to get drunk was proverbial. So great was his lung capacity that he called his men to dinner by blowing through a hollow tree a blast so strong that it blew down the timber on sixty acres, and when he spoke, the limbs sometimes fell from the trees. To keep his pipe filled required the entire time of a swamper with a scoop-shovel. At writing, however, Paul had no skill. He kept his men's time by cutting notches in a stick of wood, and he ordered supplies for camp by drawing pictures of what he wanted.

Bunyan was assisted in his lumbering exploits by a wonderful blue ox, Babe, that had the strength of nine horses, weighed at least five thousand pounds and measured from tip to tip of his horns exactly seven axe handles and a plug of tobacco. Originally Babe was pure white, but one winter in the woods it snowed blue snow for seven days (that was the winter of the snow-snakes) and from lying out in the snow all winter Babe became and remained a brilliant blue.

One tale of the blue ox is best told in the words of the lumberjack who sent it to a friend of researcher-author, Mrs. K. Bernice Stuart Campbell, in a letter written with very evident care and with every other word capitalized:

> Paul B Driving a large Bunch of logs Down the Wisconsin River When the logs Suddenly Jamed in the Dells. The logs were piled Two Hundred feet high at the head, And were backed up for One mile up river. Paul was at the rear of the Jam with the Blue Oxen And while he was coming to the front the Crew was trying to break the Jam but they couldent Budge it. When Paul Arrived at the Head with the ox he told them to Stand Back. He put the Ox in the old Wisc. in front of the Jam. And then Standing on the Bank Shot the Ox with a 303 Savage Rifle. The Ox thought it was flies And began to Switch his Tail. The tail commenced to go around in a circle And up Stream And do you know That Ox Switching his tail forced that Stream to flow Backwards And Eventually the Jam floated back Also. He took the ox out

Millions of Americans and others around the world can thank the willow (family Salix) *for acetysalicylic acid, commonly called aspirin.*

of the Stream. And let the Stream And logs go on their way.

Most of the exploits of Paul Bunyan center at Round River. Here Bunyan and his crew labored all one winter to clear the pine from a single forty. And here we'll let another one of Paul's jacks relate the tale:

As quick as the ice went out in the spring, Paul began to get ready for the drive. He had to build some dams in the stream to raise the water high enough to float his logs. But by spring he was ready for the drive. He had been training a bunch of beaver all winter; as soon as the ice went out he set those beaver to work. Just as soon as they finished one dam, he'd start them on another. It wasn't long before the dams were built.

We started out one morning and drove for two days, never seeing a sign of anyone until long after sundown of the second day, when we passed a mighty big camp. We didn't stop. We kept right on going for a couple more days when we passed another big camp. But the logs were running good and fast, so we didn't stop there either. In about two more days we came to another camp. The funny thing was that these three camps looked alot alike. Do you know that when we stopped at this third camp, it was our own camp? We had passed that camp three times. You see, we were on Round River. Round River has no beginning or end, it just runs in a circle. Well, Old Paul was in a hurry to get them logs to Muskegon; so he went out the next morning with his shovel and dug a ditch from there over to where he had plowed the furrow from Houghton Lake to Muskegon.

As soon as the drive was over, I came back home. Old Paul moved his camps to Minnesota that summer, and

Tom Myers

The rich lore of the willow goes back at least as far as ancient Greece and the nymph Helike, who was its spirit.

Legend states that the first Christmas tree was taken from amid the debris of a huge oak which had been sacred to a pagan deity.

it was too far for me to walk, so I stayed round here ever since.

Now these are some facts about Paul Bunyan's camp. I could tell you some real whoppers about Old Paul, but you must remember that I am trying to sort out the truths.

The Bunyan legends are remarkable in their quality of exaggeration, the basis of what has come to be known as typical American humor. American literary men consider these tall yarns of Paul Bunyan, giant logger, prince and hero of American lumberjacks, a home-grown Hercules, to be, with the folktales of the American Indian, the greatest contribution to American folklore.

Strange Legends

Yggdrasill, known as the World Tree, was an immense ash that Ancient Norsemen believed in. Its roots, so the story goes, were in Hel, the kingdom of death, its branches in Heaven. And the stars hung in its crown. At the base of the trees, around the sacred well, there were three Nornir, or fates. These fates decided the course of human events.

In Sweden there was a tree believed by local people to cure sickness in children and so naked youngsters would be dragged through the exposed roots of the tree by their mothers. The charm was supposed to work only on Thursdays!

California's Maidu Indians believed that originally the earth was a mass of fire which gradually collected in the center. The roots of trees were thought to be connected to the fire which could be extracted by the use of a special drill.

The willow has a rich lore going back to ancient times. In Greek mythology many trees were inhabited by spirits. The Greek nymph Helike's tree was the willow. Roman soldiers used willow for shields not only because the wood was light but perhaps also because it was thought to have some special arrow repelling properties.

The ancient Greeks knew the therapeutic values of willow and Hippocrates, the "Father of Medicine," is said to have recommend-

ed extracts of willow bark for relieving pain and fever. He was on the right track. Few of us realize that when we take an aspirin to bring relief from headache or backache that we really can thank the willow tree for this. How many millions of us who have heard the ads about pain relief from a well-known product containing "acetylsalicylic acid" know that salicylic acid got its name from *Salix,* the Latin name for willow? It is true. Experimentation that began with a substance derived from willow bark eventually led to the development of aspirin, although our modern aspirin is a synthetic product. An Alsatian chemist, Charles Frederic von Gerhardt, first compounded it in 1853, but it remained a neglected discovery until a young staff chemist named Felix Hoffman at the Friedrich Bayer Company in Düsseldorf, Germany, spurred in his search for a new and better pain killer by the sufferings of his arthritic father, found von Gerhardt's compound effective. The Bayer Company put it on the market in 1899. When the Bayer world patents expired in 1916, other companies began making and selling it. Dr. Heinrich Dreser, head of the Bayer drug research department, named it "aspirin," a coined name suggested by spirea plants which also yield an extract similar to that obtained from willows.

The famous Swedish botanist Linnaeus gave the weeping willow its name *babylonica* because it was thought to be the willow at Babylon where the exiled Jews wept. "By the rivers of Babylon, there we sat down, yea, we wept, when we remembered Zion." (Psalms 137:1)

The evergreen symbolized immortal life for the Druids of England and they are credited with being the first to hang evergreens in their homes, more than two centuries before the birth of Christ. Their neighbors in Scandinavia had a form of tree worship (and according to Sir James G. Frazer in *The Golden Bough,* so did most of the ancient European and Asian peoples). After the establishment of Christianity the Scandinavians made trees an important part of their Christmas festivals.

The Christmas tree legend as told in "The First Christmas Tree" by Henry Van Dyke, goes back to the eighth century when Winfried of England (later known as St. Boniface) brought Christianity to Germany. As with most legends, this too is a mixture of fact and myth. Like many of the early missionaries who went into strange lands to preach the gospel, the life of Winfried was one of privation and hardship. However, he was recognized in Rome in the first quarter of the eighth century by Pope Gregory II for his early work among the German people. In A.D. 722 upon his return to Germany, his adopted country, he found that Chieftain Gundhar's oldest son, Bernhard, was to be sacrificed to the gods by a forest-dwelling tribe on Christmas eve. The sacrifice was to take place at the thunder-oak of Geismar to propitiate the great Thor, god of thunder and war, to whom the oak was sacred. Winfried wanted to prove this pagan deity was powerless and was obliged to destroy the tree. He and the young man who was accompanying him, Gregor, grandson of the king, immediately and "firmly took axe-helves and swung the shining blades. . . . The huge oak quivered. There was a shuddering in the branches." And then "a strong whirling wind . . . gripped the oak . . . and tore it from the roots." Those assembled around the tree were awed by what happened. They then asked Winfried for the word of God. He told them that Jesus did not ask for human sacrifice but for service to others. He said, "This is the word, and this is the counsel. Not a drop of blood shall fall tonight . . . for this is the birth-night of Christ, Son of the All-Father and Saviour of mankind."

Looking at a young green fir tree standing straight with its top pointing to the stars, amid the debris of the fallen oak, Winfried said, "Here is the living tree, with no stain of blood upon it, that shall be the sign of your new worship. Call it the tree of the Christ-child. You shall keep it at home, with laughter and songs and rites of love. There shall not be a home where the children are not gathered around the green fir-tree to rejoice in the birth-night of Christ." It is then told that the mighty fallen oak was used to build a little chapel devoted to God and His servant Saint Peter, and that the little fir tree was cut and taken to Gundhar's great hall and set up for the observance of Christmas. This, then, according to legend, was the first Christmas tree.

In the early years of the twentieth century the White House did not have Christmas trees because Teddy Roosevelt would not approve of any cutting in U.S. forests. He was shown that forests could be improved by selective cutting and promptly re-established the Christmas tree tradition in the White House. Since T.R.'s time, foresters have shown repeatedly and conclusively that a forest can be helped by selective thinning. Today, a tree for Christmas is one of any tree's happiest uses.

Subalpine fir bole floridly weathered in California's high Sierras.

IV FAMOUS TREES

There have been no Methuselahs since the flood. Man's maximum of life is a century. Only the elephant and the tortoise feebly imitate the longevity of the antediluvians. But there are living things that outlive them all. . . . They are trees, about which memories cluster like the trailing vines. They (old ones) are not numerous, and are therefore more precious. In the shadows of the dark forests, in the light of the lofty hills, in the warmth and beauty of the broad plains of the great globe, they stand in matchless dignity as exceptions. They are Patriarchs in the society of the vegetable kingdom. . . .

With what mute eloquence do they address us. With what moving pathos do the trees of Olivet discourse of Jesus, his beautiful life and sublime death. How the cedars of Lebanon talk of Solomon and Hiram, and the great Temple of the Lord in Jerusalem. How the presence of "those green-robed senators of mighty wood" stirs the spirit of worship in the human soul!

In our own country, and in our own time, there have been, and still are, ancient trees intimately connected with our history as colonists and as a nation, and which command the reverence of every American.

from *Harper's New Monthly Magazine*
No. CXLIV. — May 1862 — Vol. XXIV
"American Historical Trees"

District fire ranger Wilbur Libby, who discovered the U.S. champion paper birch, peers over the shoulder of former Maine forest commissioner Austin Wilkins, measuring the 18' 1" girth of the 96' tall giant, near Hartford, Maine. Its crown spread is 83 feet.

TREE: THE CHARTER OAK
LOCATION: Hartford, Connecticut
HISTORY: Indians asked settlers to spare this tree because it had guided their ancestors for hundreds of years.
DIED: 1856

The Charter Oak had been a common sight to the colonists in Hartford, Connecticut, ever since their arrival in 1633. The Indians said it had been there for hundreds of years before that. But, its greatest moment was to come in 1687 when it would play a part in a mystery story. This story was best related by an article on American historical trees published in May 1862, in *Harper's* magazine, reprinted here in part:

"When James, Duke of York, one of the worst of the Stuart dynasty, ascended the British throne, he took measures, by the advice of unscrupulous courtiers, to suppress the growth of free governments in America, which had been established and fostered under liberal charters given by his brother and predecessor, Charles the Second. He conceived a scheme for making all New England a sort of vice-royalty; and he sent Edmund Andross, a bigot and petty tyrant, to take away the charters from the different colonies, and rule over them all as Governor-General. Connecticut refused to give up her charter. The incensed Andross went to Hartford with a band of soldiers, at the close of October, 1687, while the Assembly was in session, to demand an instant surrender of it. He walked into the Assembly chamber with all the assumed dignity of a Dictator. The members received him courteously. He made his demand with hauteur, and the subject was discussed with dignified freedom until evening and the candles were lighted. The charter, contained in a neat, long box, was placed upon the table. Andross stretched forth his hand to take it, when the lights were suddenly extinguished, loud huzzas went up from a large crowd outside, and many pressed into the Assembly chamber. Captain Wadsworth, according to concerted plan, had seized the charter, and borne it away in the gloom unperceived. He hid it in the cavity of a venerable oak in front of the mansion of the Honorable Samual Wyllys, a magistrate of the colony.

The candles were soon relighted, order was restored, but the charter could not be found. No one could or would reveal the place of its concealment. Andross stormed, and threatened them with the hot displeasure of the King. The members heard him with calmness, and they uttered no word of remonstrance when he took possession of their records, declared the General Court dissolved, and the Government at an end, writing *Finis* upon their journal at the close of such declaration.

They knew the value and power of their preserved Constitution.

The Charter was not long concealed. James was soon driven from the British throne, and Andross from New England. Eminent English jurists decided that as Connecticut had never surrendered its charter it remained in full force. It was drawn from its hidingplace, and the government was immediately re-established under it. From that time until its destruction Wyllys's venerable tree was known as the Charter Oak.

An interesting fact may properly be mentioned in this connection. Charles the Second granted the charter to Connecticut, which was concealed in an oak for its preservation. Charles himself was concealed in a hollow oak eleven years before (1676), for his own preservation, after the battle of Worcester. In honor of his King, and in commemoration of this event, Dr. Halley, the astronomer, named a constellation in the heavens *Robur Caroli*. The oak may be justly styled a royal tree. Spenser speaks of it as 'The builder oak, sole King of forests all.' It is an emblem of strength, constancy, virtue, and long life; attributes which ought to be the characteristics of a monarch."

from *Harper's New Monthly Magazine*
No. CXLIV.—May 1862—Vol. XXIV
"American Historical Trees"

TREE: CHAMPION LONGLEAF PINE
LOCATION: Near Hemphill, Texas
STILL LIVING

This species has the longest needles of any pine species in the United States. It's also noted for its long, straight bole of dense wood and because of this is often used for power and telephone poles. It is also valuable for pilings, lumber and paper and is frequently used for ship masts, railroad ties and flooring. Its ability to produce large quantities of gum, which yields turpentine and resin, has made the species a leading producer of naval stores in some parts of the South.

Texas contains the largest longleaf pine in the nation, a tree whose girth measured 111-1/2 inches in 1970. It was 134 feet tall that year and had a crown spread of 34 feet. Although Texas, as might be expected, claims the nation's largest tree of this species, the state has only the second smallest growth area of the nine Southern states in which *Pinus palustris* is native.

The national champion longleaf pine —
134' height, 111½" girth, 34-foot crown —
stands among a grove of peers in Pine Park,
five miles west of Hemphill, Texas.

Texas Forest Service

TREE: THE COLUMBUS COURT OAK
LOCATION: Columbus, Texas, about halfway between San Antonio and Houston
STILL LIVING

By 1837 Texas had declared itself a republic. But the declaration did not have much effect on Santa Anna and his army who were determined to squash the rebels. The rebels had the audacity to declare themselves free of Mexico's authority. General Sam Houston, the Texas leader, ordered a retreat and a scorched-earth policy. Towns were burned, including Columbus.

When Santa Anna was finally defeated the people of Columbus began to reconstruct their city. One of the first needs was a court of justice. Since no suitable building stood, court was convened under the large Columbus Court Oak tree. Robert McAlpix Williamson, called "three-legged Willie" by his enemies, was the judge. His nickname came from a disease which permanently bent his right leg at the knee. To gain greater mobility he wore a wooden leg and covered his wooden leg and real legs with three-legged trousers. One of the first cases under the tree of justice was that of a thief, William Bibbs. Williamson, feeling lenient that day, sentenced him to thirty-nine lashes, branding of the letter "T" on his right palm and court costs. Since Bibbs was indigent, Williamson waived the costs.

The famous oak is located in Columbus, Texas. Under its branches the first term of the Colorado County District Court was held in 1837.

71

Large, ancient, historical trees antedate Europeans on the North American continent.

Texas Forest Service

This champion 49' high, 41" girth Texas palmetto may have been the first palm seen by Alberto Cantino when he explored the Rio Grande River area near present-day Brownsville in 1502, which would make this the first palm seen on this continent by a European.

TREE: THE EVANGELINE OAK
LOCATION: Bayou Teche, St. Martinville, Louisiana
HISTORY: Tree grew at traditional landing place of the exiled Arcadians in America
STILL LIVING

Late in the seventeenth century, the English were victorious in a series of wars with the French to determine who would be master of Canada and America. The original French settlers of Arcadia, now known as Nova Scotia, were exiled to Maryland and Louisiana. Longfellow's poem, "Evangeline," is based on the legend of Emmeline Labiche who emigrated to Maryland while her lover went to Louisiana. Heartbroken, she traveled to Louisiana and found her lover beneath this oak — now one of America's most famous trees.

TREE: CHAMPION TEXAS PALMETTO
LOCATION: Eight miles southeast of Brownsville, Texas
STILL LIVING

Eleven years before Ponce de Leon's exploration of the Southwest, another explorer, Alberto Cantino, came to this area of Texas. A map drawn by him in 1502 called what we now know as the Rio Grande the Rio de las Palmas, the River of Palms. This tree is on the southernmost bend of the river and probably was the first one seen by Cantino. This champion tree is 49 feet high with a 41-inch trunk circumference and a twelve-foot crown. It is on the Rabb Plantation, which is now owned by the Audubon Society. This tree may have been the first palm sighted on the North American continent by a European.

TREE: HENDRICK HUDSON'S TREE
LOCATION: Inwood Park, Manhattan, New York
HISTORY: This tulip tree or yellow poplar greeted Hudson upon his exploration of the Hudson River
STILL LIVING

Manhattan's skyline almost seems to change by the hour as old buildings tumble and new ones rise to take their place. Today Hendrick Hudson probably would not recognize this island in the mouth of his namesake river. Legend says that in 1609 Hudson met with Indians beneath a tree which now bears his name — Hendrick Hudson's Tree — on the bank of the Harlem River, just before it joins the Hudson. Today the explorer might recognize only massive Central Park or tiny, half-mile square Inwood Park where the tree is located.

The first treaty with the Susquehannock Indians was made under the Liberty poplar in 1862. The tree was then well over a century old.

TREE: THE LIBERTY TREE
LOCATION: Annapolis, Maryland
HISTORY: First treaty signed with Susquehannock Indians
AGE: 400 years old — still living

The Liberty Tree, a giant tulip poplar, is thought to be the oldest living "thing" in the Eastern part of this country. The first treaty with the Susquehannock Indians was made under this giant tree in 1682. During the Revolutionary War, patriots of Annapolis assembled and drilled here. After the war, people gathered near and under it to celebrate peace tidings. General Lafayette was entertained under this giant tree in 1825 on the occasion of an official visit to Annapolis. The tree has a spread of 83 feet, is 114 feet high and has a circumference of 26 feet, 1 inch at 4-1/2 feet. A plaque indicates the tree is over six hundred years old but this has been questioned by some authorities and at least one increment boring resulted in a placement of age at about four hundred years.

TREE: THE PINE CREEK ELM
LOCATION: On the shores of Pine Creek (Tiadaghton Creek) near Clinton, Pennsylvania
HISTORY: Sometimes called the Liberty Tree, it witnessed Pennsylvania woodsmen declaring themselves independent of England
STILL LIVING

In 1776 the winds of freedom blew west from Boston and Philadelphia to the newly settled territories. There the independent, freedom loving farmers and woodsmen chafed under British rule. On July 4, 1776, a group of Pennsylvania pioneers gathered under the Pine Creek Elm and declared themselves free of English rule. They wrote their own declaration of independence and sent it to Philadelphia to show support of the Revolution.

TREE: THE WASHINGTON ELM
LOCATION: Cambridge, Massachusetts
HISTORY: The Washington Elm, sometimes known as the Cambridge Elm, spread its shady boughs over George Washington on July 3, 1775, as he took command of the Continental Army
DIED: October 1923

The thunder-peal of revolution that went forth from Lexington and Concord aroused all New England, and a formidable army was soon gathered around Boston, with a determination to confine the British invader to that peninsula or drive him into the sea. The storm cloud of war grew more portentous every hour. At length it burst upon Bunker Hill, and the great conflict for American independence began. The patriots looked for a competent captain to lead them to absolute freedom and peace. That commander was found in George Washington of Virginia. A New England delegate suggested him, a Maryland delegate nominated him, and the Confederate Congress appointed him commander-in-chief of all "the Continental forces raised or to be raised for the defense of American liberty." The army at Boston was adopted as the army of the nation; and on the 21st day of June, 1775, Washington left Philadelphia for the New England capital to take command of it. He arrived at Cambridge, and made his headquarters there on the 2nd of July. He was accompanied by Major General Lee, his next in command, and other officers, and received the most enthusiastic greetings from the people on the way.

At about nine o'clock on the morning of the 3rd of July, Washington, accompanied by the general officers of the army who were present, proceeded on foot from the quarters of the commander-in-chief to a great elm tree at the north end of Cambridge Common, near which the Republican forces were drawn up in proper order. Under the shadow of that wide-spreading tree, Washington stepped forward a few paces, made some appropriate remarks, drew his sword, and formally assumed the command of the army.

Eighty-six years have passed away since that imposing and important event occurred. The great elm tree is still there, flourishing in the pride of its strength and beauty. Near it, when I sketched it in 1848, was Moore's house, one of the oldest in Cambridge, in which then lived the venerable Mrs. Moore, who saw the ceremony from the window of that dwelling. The venerable elm stands there in the midst of a busy city, a living representative of the forest that covered the land when the Pilgrim Fathers came.

from *Harper's New Monthly Magazine*
No. CXLIV. — May 1862 — Vol. XXIV
"American Historical Trees"

TREE: THE LANIER OAK
LOCATION: Edge of the marshes of Glynn, near Brunswick, Glynn County, Georgia
HISTORY: Inspired Sidney Lanier to write "The Marshes of Glynn"
AGE: Over 300 years old — still living

A bronze plate under the Lanier Oak marks the place where Sidney Lanier was inspired to write his most beloved poem, "The Marshes of Glynn." Lanier (1842-1881) enlisted in the Confederate Army in November 1864, was captured aboard a blockade runner and imprisoned in Point Lookout, Maryland, for three months. He remained in the Baltimore area for most of his remaining years and there wrote "Tiger Lilies," a novel of his wartime experiences. He is buried in Baltimore's Greenmount cemetery.

TREE: LOGAN ELM
LOCATION: Logan Elm State Memorial, near Circleville, Ohio
HISTORY: Famous Indian orator, Logan, made his speech beneath this tree
Died about 1963

By 1700, the New England colonies were flourishing. Many were satisfied to stay in the civilized world of colonial America, but others decided to seek their fortunes west of the Appalachians. As they settled in the West, they seized lands which the Indians considered theirs by tradition and treaty. In what is now the State of Ohio, settlers and Indians engaged in guerilla warfare. The Shawnees, under Chief Cornstalk, had formed a confederacy of tribes to carry on the war. However, Logan, Chief of the Mingoes and a friend of the white settlers, did not participate in wars until his sister and other relatives were killed in a raid. Logan then swore vengeance and he and his tribe joined the war.

At the Battle of Point Pleasant on October 10, 1774, the Indians were defeated. A peace parley was called, but Logan refused to attend. A white scout, John Gibson, sought him out and found him under a large elm. Thereafter historically the tree was known as the

Logan, chief of the Mingo Indians, was found by whites in October 1774, sitting under this elm after he unsuccessfully had sought peace for himself and his people.

Logan Elm, and it lived until about 1963. Logan wanted peace and realized that if he did not honor the treaty, the war would continue. So, he sent this message through Gibson:

> I appeal to any white man to say, if he ever entered Logan's cabin hungry and he gave him not meat; if ever he came cold and naked, and he clothed him not. During the course of the last long and bloody war Logan remained idle in his cabin, an advocate for peace. Such was my love for the whites that my countrymen pointed as they passed and said, "Logan is a friend of white men." I had even thought to have lived with you, but for the injuries of one man. Colonel Cresap, the last spring, in cold blood and unprovoked, murdered all the relations of Logan, not even sparing my women and children. There runs not a drop of my blood in the veins of any living creature. This called on me for revenge. I have sought it: I have killed many: I have fully gutted my vengeance: for my country I rejoice at the beams of peace. But do not harbor a thought that mine is the joy of fear. Logan never felt fear. He will not turn his heel to save his life. Who is there to mourn for Logan? Not one.

TREE: THE JUDGMENT TREE
LOCATION: Nathan Boone Homestead, Femme Osage Creek, near Defiance, St. Charles County, Missouri
HISTORY: Daniel Boone held court beneath this tree
STILL ALIVE

In the days when Spain still ruled the Louisiana Territory, of which Missouri was a part, Daniel Boone became a Syndic for the Spanish government, an office somewhat like our justice of the peace. He often held court beneath the Judgment Tree, a broad substantial American elm, on his son's homestead. One of Boone's cases involved beaver trapping rights on the LaCharette Creek in what is now Warren County. Indians complained that the white men were eradicating the beaver on the creek. Boone settled the matter by giving trapping rights to the Indians on one side of the creek and to the whites on the other side. The beavers weren't aware of this treaty and were soon extinct.

*Daniel Boone, as judge, once held court under this broad elm.
In one of the cases he gave Indians the right to trap beaver on one
side of a stream, whites the opposite side. Not knowing of
the treaty, the beavers were quickly wiped out.*

TREE: THE SYCAMORE WHICH OWNED ITSELF
LOCATION: Alice Lloyd College, Caney Creek, Pippa Passes, Kentucky
HISTORY: In reward for providing shade and inspiration, the tree was given possession of itself
AGE: 1790-1941

The deed relates in part:

> For, and in consideration of its shade, coolness, and inspiration, and in value of itself as an aesthetic asset, the parties of the first part (Mrs. Lloyd, as trustee for the Caney Creek Community Center) hereby convey to the party of the second part in trust for the use and benefit of the said sycamore tree, and to *itself* as absolute owner, the said tree, and the said terra firma, the ground upon which it stands is to belong to *itself*, and is hereby conveyed in the same manner as the said tree is conveyed, in consideration of the value of itself as a resting place for the weary under the shade of said tree; and the said tree and the said terra firma are to belong to themselves absolutely and to each other for all the purposes which Nature and God intended, among which is the purpose of the soil to nurture and feed the tree, and that of the tree to shade, grace and beautify the said terra firma.

The 150-year-old sycamore, located on the campus of Alice Lloyd College on Caney Creek at Pippa Passes, Kentucky, was 156 feet tall and twelve feet, five inches in circumference.

TREE: MAGNOLIA COUNCIL TREE
LOCATION: Charleston, South Carolina
SIZE: Branches spread over a space of more than 200 square feet
CUT DOWN: 1849

I was in Charleston, South Carolina, early in 1849, and rode out toward evening to the remains of the lines of fortifications thrown across the Neck during the Revolution. It was just at sunset when we rode through an avenue of live oaks draped with moss, and visited the ruins of the magazine, officers' quarters, and other structures of that period, about four miles from the city. On our way, a mile and a half nearer the town, we turned aside to see a venerable and magnificent magnolia tree, under which, according to well-sustained tradition, General Lincoln held a council with his officers and leading citizens of Charleston during the siege of that place by the British in 1780.

It was on the 21st day of April — a bright and sultry day; and there, in the open air, in the shade of that noble Magnolia, close by the quaint cottage of Colonel William Cummington, they discussed the propriety of an attempted retreat of the army to the open country. Sir Henry Clinton, who had carried on the siege for several weeks, had just been reinforced by Lord Cornwallis with three thousand troups from New York. The city would be speedily blockaded by sea and land, and there was no hope of safety for the army but in flight. The representatives of the inhabitants objected to its departure, because they feared the exasperation of the enemy after suffering such obstinate resistance. Lincoln remained, and three weeks afterward the army and city were surrendered to the British.

This beautiful Council Tree, as it was called, was ever held in special veneration by the loyal inhabitants of Charleston. Its branches, at the time of my visit, had spread over a space of more than two hundred square feet. But on that very day the indolent owner, displaying the absence of the nobler sensibilities of the human heart, had cut it down for firewood!

from *Harper's New Monthly Magazine*
No. CXLIV. — May 1862 — Vol. XXIV
"American Historical Trees"

TREE: TEACH'S OAK
LOCATION: Near Ocracoke Inlet on the North Carolina Outer Banks near the village of Oriental
HISTORY: Pirate treasure is believed to be buried near this tree
STILL LIVING

Edward Teach, Blackbeard the Pirate, plundered ships along the Virginia and Carolina coasts in the early 1700's. Legend has it that Teach's Oak, long used as a landmark by sailors, attracted Blackbeard and he used the Ocracoke inlet on the North Carolina shore as a refuge. Many believe he buried his booty beneath the Teach Oak. But although many have searched for it, the legendary treasure has not yet been found.

TREE: GEORGIA PEACH TREE
LOCATION: Throughout Georgia

There is no "one and only" Georgia peach tree. An Indian village called Standing Peachtree was flourishing in 1782, according to a military dispatch. It was located at the Chattahoochee River and Peachtree Creek. Fort Peachtree was built there in 1814. Since the peach is a short-lived tree, none can be

The old cedar stands on Kershaw Courthouse grounds and is said to have been planted by the Marquis de LaFayette in 1825.

old, he took it to a show at Louisiana, Missouri. The Stark Nursery representative at the show took one bite, exclaimed, and at the same time named the apple, "Delicious." Over the years, over eight million grafts were made from this parent tree and its scions to make it the most popular eating apple in America. The original tree died, but a monument marks where it grew.

TREE: LAFAYETTE CEDAR
LOCATION: Camden, South Carolina
HISTORY: Planted by Lafayette
STILL LIVING

This old cedar is said to have been planted by the Marquis de Lafayette when he visited Camden in 1825. On the grounds of the Kershaw Courthouse, which has been rebuilt several times, the Lafayette Cedar still stands.

TREE: THE MINGO OAK
LOCATION: Trace Creek Valley, Mingo County, West Virginia
HISTORY: The greatest white oak known to man
AGE: 1361-1938

The Mingo white oak stood over 200 feet high, the greatest recorded white oak known to man. The first 145 feet of this height was free of branches. Above this graceful column a crown of branches grew, 130 feet in diameter and 60 feet high. So awe inspiring was this great tree, that a pulpit was set up next to it and ministers would come to preach there before a congregation of mountaineers.

For six hundred years, this tree withstood the ravages of nature, only to fall to the hand of man. It is said the tree died of suffocation from the fumes of mining wastes. It was cut down in 1938 and an attempt was made to preserve its ten-foot-diameter stump. But even this stump is now fast deteriorating. Portions of the oak were sent to the Smithsonian Institution. This oak was 131 years old when Columbus discovered the New World; 203 years old during the Elizabethan Age; 259 years when the Pilgrims landed at Plymouth Rock and 415 years when the Declaration of Independence was signed.

TREE: THE FRIENDSHIP TREE
LOCATION: Bath, Pennsylvania
HISTORY: This horsechestnut was given to one another by three famous Americans
DIED

Giving a living thing as a gift of friendship is a long tradition. Today, we give flowers to a special friend or on special occasions. The

singled out for historical reference, but that does not detract from its beauty and wonderful fruit it bears.

TREE: THE DELICIOUS APPLE TREE
LOCATION: Winterset, Madison County, Iowa
HISTORY: Parent tree to all Delicious apple trees
DIED

Jesse Hiatt was a man, his neighbors said, who was not content to leave well enough alone. In his quest to find something better, he grafted a Yellow Bellflower sprout onto a Vermont apple seedling and planted it on his Winthrop, Iowa, farm. The result was a bigger, better and tastier apple than had ever been seen before. Jesse was so proud of this apple that, although he was almost seventy years

Friendship Tree was given to General George Washington by "Lighthorse Harry" Lee, the father of Robert E. Lee. Washington intended to plant it at Mount Vernon, but later decided to give it as a gift of friendship to a member of his Continental Army staff, General Robert Brown, who planted it in front of his home in Bath, Pennsylvania. To perpetuate the friendship of these three men, seeds of the tree have been presented for planting at state capitols and universities.

TREE: THE BIG IOWA SYCAMORE
LOCATION: Near the town of Red Rock, Marion County, Iowa
HISTORY: It grows in an area rich in Indian artifacts, dating from the time of the mound-building Indians
STILL LIVING

The centuries-old big Iowa sycamore trunk spans 23 feet in circumference at shoulder height. It is the second largest sycamore in the country, exceeded only by an Ohio sycamore with a 42-foot, 7-inch trunk circumference. The exact age of the tree is not known, but it is certain that the tree witnessed a procession of Indians, the Sioux, Iowas, Potawatomies, Winnebagoes, Sac and Foxes, pass by and, relatively recently, the coming of the white man. The tree was old when the first steamboats came to Des Moines in 1837 and occasioned the development of Red Rock, Iowa, into a bustling, lawless river frontier town in the 1840's.

TREE: THE KIT CARSON PINE
LOCATION: Carson's Pass, Sierra Nevada Mountains, California
HISTORY: Frontiersman Kit Carson cut his name into this pine
DIED: 1888

When the '49ers headed to "California or bust" they faced many obstacles. First, the seemingly endless prairies. Then the Rocky Mountains, followed by the salt-caked deserts of Utah. Finally, an obstacle unexpected by many, the Sierra Nevada Mountains, the last barrier to the California gold fields. This mountain range would have stopped these pioneers except for the passes marked out by men like Kit Carson. While guiding Captain John C. Frémont on a government exploration, Carson inscribed his name on a pine at the summit of the pass he discovered. Forty-four years later, the tree was cut down and the section bearing Carson's name sent to Sutter's Fort, Sacramento. A replica of the inscription is now in the California capitol.

TREE: BATTLE GROUND OAK
LOCATION: Near Guilford Courthouse, Greensborough, North Carolina
HISTORY: This tree witnessed what many historians believe to be the fulcrum of the Revolutionary War
STILL LIVING

It is sometimes said that a country may lose all the battles, but win the war. The Battle of Guilford Courthouse in North Carolina was such a battle for the struggling American colonies. Nathaniel Greene, an American general, tied his horse to the Battle Ground Oak and directed the battle. The British won, but at such a high price that many believe it led to their defeat and ultimate surrender at Yorktown a few months later in October 1781. The multitude of branches from the top of the tree are said to have been caused by General Greene's horse, who nipped the top of the young tree while he was tethered to it.

TREE: THE BIG TREE (AN OAK)
LOCATION: Bank of the Genesee River near the village of Geneseo, New York
SIZE: Trunk was twenty-six feet nine inches in circumference
AGE: Estimated to be over a thousand years old when it was swept away by a flood in November 1857

Probably the most ancient of these living links of the present with the past was The Big Tree that stood on the bank of the Genesee River, near the village of Geneseo, New York. When the white man first saw it it was the patriarch of the Genesee Valley, and was so revered by the Senecas that they named the beautiful savanna around it and their village near it "Big Tree." It also gave name to an eminent Seneca chief, the coadjutor and friend of Corn-planter, Half-town, Farmers-brother, and other great leaders of the warlike Seneca nation, when Sullivan, with a chastising army, swept so ruthlessly through their beautiful land in the early autumn of 1779.

The Big Tree was an oak; and when, with a small party, I visited and sketched it in the summer of 1857, a few weeks before its destruction, its appearance was a fair counterpart of another thus described by Spenser:

> A huge oak, dry and dead,
> Still clad with reliques of its trophies old;
> Lifting to heaven its aged, hoary head;
> Whose feet on earth, had got but feeble hold,
> And half-disboweled stands above the ground,
> With wreathed roots and naked arms.

We measured the trunk, and found it to be twenty-six feet nine inches in circumference.

Its age was doubtless more than a thousand years. During a great flood in the Genesee River, early in November, 1857, The Big Tree was swept away, and buried in the bosom of Lake Ontario.

from *Harper's New Monthly Magazine*
No. CXLIV. — May 1862 — Vol. XXIV
"American Historical Trees"

TREE: WASHINGTON OAK
LOCATION: Hampton Plantation, South Carolina
HISTORY: Washington reportedly said about the oak, "Let the tree stand."
STILL ALIVE: On Hampton Plantation which is in the process of being partially acquired by the State of South Carolina for a historical park

This large, live oak is on Hampton Plantation, former home of Archibald Rutledge, poet laureate of South Carolina. When George Washington was touring the South in 1791, he decided to visit Mrs. Daniel Horry, great-great-grandmother of Rutledge. In the course of a conversation with Washington, Mrs. Horry asked which trees should be left and which removed to improve the plantation yard. Washington pointed to the oak and said, "Let the tree stand." A bronze plaque placed there by the Daughters of the American Revolution commemorates that event.

TREE: THOMASVILLE,GEORGIA,BIG OAK
LOCATION: Thomasville, Georgia
SIZE: 22 feet in circumference as of 1964
AGE: 288 years old — still living

This live oak, with a trunk twenty-two feet in circumference, is a member of a very exclusive club, the Live Oak Society, which seeks "the preservation of these ancient giants of our forests." To be eligible for membership, a tree must have celebrated its 100th birthday. Dues of twenty-five acorns a year must be paid to continue listing on the active membership roster. The Society was organized in 1935 at the University of Southwestern Louisiana. Live oaks in Mississippi, Alabama, Florida, South Carolina, Texas and Louisiana are also members.

TREE: TURNER RED CEDAR
LOCATION: Eastern Texas, north of the Galveston, Port Arthur area
HISTORY: Second largest of its kind in America
STILL LIVING

This red cedar shades a house built in 1835 by Ruffin C. Turner, who came to Texas from North Carolina. The house still stands on the

George Washington admired this oak in 1791. Asked his advice on which trees to cull or save for plantation improvement, Washington specified this tree for preservation.

South Carolina State Commission of Forestry

*This huge cedar in 1835 witnessed
the building of the house it still shades on
a 4,605 - acre grant of land north of Galveston.*

Turner grant which was made up of a league, 4,428 acres, and a labor, 177 acres, of land in what is now Jasper County, Texas.

TREE: THE BEN MILAM CYPRESS
LOCATION: Near the Alamo, San Antonio, Texas
HISTORY: Mexican army snipers fired at the Alamo from this tree when Texans went to the San Antonio River for water
STILL LIVING

In December 1835, Texans and Mexicans fought for possession of this new land in the Southwest. General Cos and his Mexican army occupied San Antonio. General Edward Burleson was sent to drive Cos out. Ben Milam

*A shot by a Mexican sniper hidden in
the tall cypress killed Ben Milam, a U.S. private,
when he went to the river for water.*

had recently escaped from Mexico, and his imprisonment gave him a good reason to want to see the Mexicans out of Texas. He joined Burleson's army as a private. On December 7, Milam entered the area between the Veramendi Palace and the river to talk to Francis W. Johnson. As he crossed the courtyard, where he thought the high walls would protect him, a sniper concealed in the large, towering tree drew careful aim, fired, and killed him instantly. Milam did not live to see the victory of Burleson's troops four days later.

TREE: WORLD'S LARGEST LIVING CHRISTMAS TREE
LOCATION: Wilmington, North Carolina
AGE: 300 years old — still living

The largest living Christmas tree is not a variety of evergreen, but a water oak, estimated to be over three hundred years old. This 75-foot-tall tree has a 210-foot limb spread that has been decorated every year since 1929. Five tons of Spanish moss and over 4,500 lights are used to decorate this tree, under which choral groups sing Christmas carols. A Santa Claus and a Nativity scene are beneath its branches.

Overleaf: *The world's largest living Christmas tree,
Wilmington, North Carolina.*
Hugh Morton: Wilmington, North Carolina, Chamber of Commerce

Texas Forest Service

81

TREE: THE RIO FRIO LANDMARK TREE
LOCATION: Northwest of San Antonio and north of Ulvalde, Texas
HISTORY: This live oak was used as a central point in laying out the town of Rio Frio
STILL LIVING

In 1866 the Lombardy Trading Company dug an irrigation ditch near this central Texas town. The company also constructed a private school, known as Lombardy Academy. The town outgrew its original name of "the Ditch" by 1871 and the new post office proudly marked its mail, "Rio Frio." N. W. Patterson used the large Rio Frio Landmark Tree as a bearing point from which the town was laid out. This was natural since many social and religious events were held under its shade. The second bearing point Patterson used was the high point on Schoolhouse Mountain to the east.

Pecan tree (right) planted by Sam Houston in 1847 at his home in Huntsville, Texas.

The Rio Frio tree (below) served as a bearing point from which a Texas town was laid out.

TREE: THE HOUSTON PECAN
LOCATION: The Sam Houston home in Huntsville, Texas
HISTORY: Planted by Sam Houston in 1847
STILL LIVING

Sam Houston was in a hurry to get to his favorite house in Huntsville, but his horse was

Texas Forest Service

Texas Forest Service

not. Sam finally had enough of the dawdling dapple and reached for his buggy whip, but it was gone. Out of frustration, he pulled the buggy to a stop and looked around. He saw what he wanted, a sapling with plenty of spring in it to inspire the horse to greater efforts. He yanked the sapling out of the ground, jumped back into the buggy, and put the impromptu whip to good use. Arriving home, he found the roots still intact on his new-found horse accelerator, so he planted it and it grew. It stands today in the south corner of the spacious Houston yard, still bearing fruit.

TREE: THE COUNCIL OAK
LOCATION: Riverside Park, Sioux City, Iowa
HISTORY: This tree shades a traditional Indian council area
STILL LIVING

This gnarled oak was over two hundred years old when Lewis and Clark camped under it in 1804 to counsel with the Indians about their proposed exploration of the Missouri River. Standing on the Missouri River bottom near the mouth of the Big Sioux River, this burr oak had looked upon councils of Indian chiefs and war parties for years before Lewis and Clark had come. The last great Indian council held under its branches was in 1854 when Smutty Bear called the leaders of the tribes to discuss white surveyors in the area. The Council Oak is nearly a hundred feet high with a trunk four feet in diameter.

South Carolina State Department of Forestry

Five South Carolina governors, including James F. Byrnes, are buried near the base of the Sire Oak at Columbia, South Carolina.

TREE: THE WESLEY OAK
LOCATION: St. Simon's Island, Georgia
HISTORY: John Wesley preached beneath this tree
STILL LIVING

American history is filled with individuals who came to this country to escape religious persecution. John Wesley, a clergyman in the Church of England, protested against some of the practices of the state religion of England and he and his brother, Charles, were forced to flee. Governor Ogelthorpe invited them to come to Georgia. The Wesley Oak witnessed the preaching of John and Charles to the British soldiers quartered on St. Simon's Island in 1736. In 1737 John returned to England to continue the work which has made him famous as a founding father of Methodism.

TREE: SIRE OAK
LOCATION: Trinity Church graveyard, opposite the Statehouse, Columbia, South Carolina
HISTORY: South Carolina statesmen buried beneath it
STILL LIVING

The large Sire Oak stands across the street from the South Carolina Statehouse, in the Trinity Church graveyard. At or near its base lie the bodies of five of South Carolina's governors: Richard Irving Manning, Wade Hampton, Hugh Smith Thompson, Richard T. Manning and James F. Byrnes.

TREE: THE TREATY OAK
LOCATION: Austin, Texas
HISTORY: Indians regarded this tree as having a mystical power. It is believed to be over 500 years old
STILL LIVING

Long before white settlers came to Texas, the Tejus, Apache and Comanche Indians held this stately oak in reverence. Love potions were brewed from its leaves. If a tea made from its leaves was drunk by a warrior under a full moon, he would return safely from war. The Treaty Oak tree is the sole survivor of a grove of oaks, known as the Council Oaks, under which Stephen F. Austin signed the first boundary agreement with the Indians. In 1927 the short-trunked tree with noble crown and spreading branches was nominated to the American Forestry Association's Hall of Fame for Trees in Washington, D.C., where it was pronounced the most perfect specimen of a North American tree. In 1937, the tree's owner wanted to cut it down, but citizen interest caused the city to buy the land as a park. The Port Arthur, Texas, Campfire Girls were one of the first contributors to a fund to save the tree.

TREE: CHAMPION MONTEZUMA BALD-CYPRESS
LOCATION: Near McAllen, Texas, on the Rio Grande River in the southernmost area of Texas
HISTORY: This variety of cypress is found only in two counties of Texas in the Lower Rio Grande Valley and in northeastern Mexico
STILL LIVING

Cypress trees were once common in North America and Europe but today only three species remain and they are all located in North America. *Taxodium distichum* (common baldcypress) is found in the southeastern United States. *T. ascenden* (pond cypress) grows in clay bottom swamps from Virginia to Florida and west to Alabama. *T. mucronatum* is found only in Hidalgo and Cameron counties in southern Texas. Commonly known as the Montezuma Baldcypress, this champion tree has a trunk circumference of 222 inches, a height of 45 feet and a crown spread of 74 feet.

TREE: HANGMANS OR TORY OAK
LOCATION: Ashley Avenue, Charleston, South Carolina
HISTORY: The site of instant justice in colonial Carolina
DIED: 1972

This large live oak stood in the middle of Ashley Avenue in Charleston, South Carolina. Enemies of the struggling revolutionaries are said to have been hanged from the Hangmans Oak tree which was also used to execute pirates.

TREE: THE DE SOTO OAK
LOCATION: University of Tampa Campus, Tampa, Florida
HISTORY: Legend has it that the Spanish explorer de Soto rested beneath this oak.
AGE: 150 years old — still living

Fernando de Soto was appointed governor of Cuba and Florida in 1539. He and about 1,000 young, wealthy Spaniards set out to explore this new world. He landed at Tampa Bay, and

Pirates and enemies of the American Revolution were hanged from this oak.

South Carolina State Department of Forestry

conferred with Indians about his proposed exploration, which would take him to the Mississippi River. According to old Indian legends the adventurous Spaniard, on his first trip to the shores of the bay, rested in the shade of this great tree. About 350 years later, General Nelson A. Miles established a headquarters beneath the De Soto Oak during the Spanish-American War in 1898.

TREE: THE LONE TREE
LOCATION: Near town of Lone Tree, midway between the Iowa and Cedar rivers in Johnson County, Iowa
HISTORY: A single elm tree in the midst of a featureless prairie
Died several years ago

The monotony of the prairies was oppressive to the pioneer as he plodded west. Nothing broke the featureless plain until the travelers came upon this elm tree, which was forty-nine inches in diameter. Even the Indians enjoyed the rest and shade it provided and named it *Ne-Te-Qui*, the Lone Tree. It is a mystery how this solitary sentinel grew here or how it survived the frequent prairie fires. It was used as a survey landmark in plotting the town of Lone Tree. Today a dead snag remains which is forty-nine inches in diameter, breast high.

TREE: THE CONSTITUTIONAL ELM
LOCATION: The banks of the Big Indian Creek, near Corydon, Indiana
HISTORY: Indiana's constitution was drafted beneath this tree and the first state capitol was located near the tree in 1816
DIED: The stump is encased in a stone shrine with a descriptive marker

In 1816, thirteen counties of the Indiana Territory were allowed to form a state government. Forty-three representatives left their homes in the Indiana wilderness and traveled to the state capitol at Corydon. These backwoodsmen felt confined in the building selected for their meetings, so they moved to the shade of a stately old elm, now the Constitutional Elm. After twenty days of deliberation there, Indiana's first constitution was drafted on June 29, 1816.

TREE: GREEN TREE HOTEL
LOCATION: Le Claire, Iowa
HISTORY: William F. Cody ("Buffalo Bill") played beneath it as a boy. A monument to him was placed beneath the tree
STILL LIVING

An early example, on Queen Anne Tree, of tree bark defacing.

In the days before the Civil War, Mississippi rivermen would rest beneath an elm near Le Claire, Iowa. Hard working men are always grateful for a cool place to rest, and, because some would camp there for days or weeks while waiting for a riverboat heading home, they jokingly named this tree the Green Tree Hotel.

TREE: QUEEN ANNE TREE
LOCATION: Ridgeway, South Carolina
STILL LIVING

This old beech has the words, "Queen Anne 1702," carved into its base. The exact age of the tree is not known, but beeches sometimes live to be three hundred years old.

TREE: THE MARK TWAIN OAK
LOCATION: Jackass Hill, Tuolomne County, California
HISTORY: Twain wrote much of his story, "The Jumping Frog of Calaveras County," beneath this oak
Died about 10 years ago

Samuel Clemens' first love was the Mississippi River, and he hoped to be a river pilot. But, shortly before the outbreak of the Civil War, the lure of California gold called him and his brother, Orion, west. He was not successful at gold mining, and he turned to journalism. He became a member of a witty group that wrote during America's literary "Golden Era" of the late nineteenth century, which included Artemus Ward and Charles W. Stoddard. While relaxing under this oak, he was inspired to write many of his famous stories.

TREE: PANNA MARIA OAKS
LOCATION: Panna Maria, Texas, about midway between San Antonio and Corpus Christi, Texas
HISTORY: These oaks mark location of first Polish settlement in America
STILL LIVING

The year is 1854. The fertile wheat fields of Poland have been fought over by the Russian bear to the east and the Prussian wolf to the west. Polish culture, which boasted of a constitutional monarchy (when the Picts of England were still painting themselves blue) and a university in Krakow (which was hundreds of years old when Columbus discovered the New World), was prostrate.

About eight hundred Polish emigrants boarded ship in Europe and headed toward the west. After nine weeks aboard ship and three weeks more of travel on foot they arrived in mid-winter at the junction of the San Antonio and Cibolo rivers. Time became blurred during the journey, but someone remembered that it must be Christmas. So, these emigrants gathered under the shelter of these small, outspread oaks, while a young priest said a mass of joy and thanksgiving for these new Americans. By the end of the first year, many of the original emigrants had moved on, but not before a small community and a church had been built beneath these Panna Maria Oaks.

TREE: THE DEAM OAK
LOCATION: Near Bluffton, Indiana
HISTORY: Only tree of its species known in U.S.
STILL LIVING

The Deam Oak located near Bluffton, Indiana, is a hybrid between a white oak and a Chinquaquin oak and is the only tree of the species known in the United States. The tree was discovered in 1904 (and is still standing) and was named for Charles C. Deam, a long time state forester. It is 85 feet high, has a circumference of 8 feet and a spread of 50 feet.

TREE: THE SALEM OAK
LOCATION: Salem, New Jersey
HISTORY: It was flourishing when the first settlers come to New England
SIZE: 20 feet in circumference
STILL LIVING

Great moments in history are played under the branches of some trees while other trees silently witness the passing of peoples and communities. An example of the latter is the Salem Oak. In the five centuries it took to grow to 90 feet in height and 20 feet in circumference, it spread its boughs over a quarter of an acre, it watched the coming of the Society of Friends (Quakers) to the New World, the drilling of the Continental Army and later the Union Army. Perhaps its most important role was to stand as a guardian and then memorial to the Society of Friends, many of whom rest beneath its shade.

TREE: INDIAN MARKER TREE
LOCATION: Door County, Wisconsin
HISTORY: Bent by Indians to mark trail
STILL LIVING

The Indian Marker maple on Chamber Island in Door County, Wisconsin, is a good example of the way the early Indians used to bend young saplings to mark a trail.

Philip Van Blaricum; Indiana Department of Natural Resources

The only tree of its species in the U.S., the Deam Oak near Bluffton, Indiana, is a hybrid white oak and Chinquaquin oak.

The massive elm at Neenah, Wisconsin, was well known as a council assembly ground for chiefs of Indian tribes.

TREE: OLD COUNCIL TREE
LOCATION: Neenah, Wisconsin
HISTORY: Treaty signed in 1819 with Winnebago Indians
CUT DOWN: 1890

This immense elm located in Neenah, Wisconsin, was used for years as a guide to steamboat pilots on Lake Winnebago. It was also well known as a council gathering place for the chiefs of neighboring Indian tribes, and a treaty was entered into under it in about 1819 between Colonel Henry Leavenworth and the Winnebago Chief Four Legs. When the channel of the river was widened in 1890 the tree was cut down. Over one hundred years ago the English poet William Blake wisely observed that "The tree which moves some to tears of joy is in the eyes of others only a green thing which stands in the way."

TREES: GENERAL SHERMAN
LOCATION: Sequoia National Park, California
SIZE: 32.2 feet in diameter
AGE: About 3,000 years — still living

The General Sherman, General Grant, and Grizzly Giant, all giant Sierra redwoods *(Sequoia gigantea)* growing on the western slopes of the Sierra Nevada in California, are the earth's biggest form of life, although the coast redwoods *(S. sempervirens)* are taller. The General Sherman in Sequoia National Park is the largest of all trees: 101 feet in circumference at the base, 273 feet high, and its weight has been estimated at 2,145 tons. Another redwood giant is the Founders Tree, tallest known tree in the world. It is 364 feet high and is located just north of Weott on the Redwood Highway.

Overleaf: *The well-known, wind-shaped Jeffrey pine on top of Sentinel Dome in Yosemite National Park, California.*
Ed Cooper

V TREES ACROSS THE LAND

Trees in any landscape, at any hour of the day or night, inform the place and time with beauty, and the man who is unaware of it is perhaps unaware of all other natural beauty and is not living his life at its fullest and best, for trees help put man in a natural perspective upon the universal face.

August Derleth

America today is a land of mobility. Few of us live out our lifetimes as our grandparents often did, within a few miles of our birthplace. Formal education is seldom concluded in a schoolhouse a mile or two down a country road but more often a thousand or more miles from home, down an interstate highway. A first job is just as apt to be on an opposite coast as the opposite corner of one's hometown or even home state. Thousands of families move back and forth across the land each year, traveling the company promotion and transfer circuit.

Transported from one part of the country to another, we often find that some trees indigenous to our new home are brand new to us. Sometimes familiar trees are missed almost as much as familiar faces. A spruce or balsam shipped at Christmas to a Midwesterner living in Florida or Arizona has been known to stir nostalgia in strong men.

Many of us have happy childhood memories of trees. A tree was to climb, to hang upside down from, to swing under in a rubber tire, or to build a tree house in, with an entrance ladder that could be pulled up as a protection from animals and other dangers of the wild.

Smell often calls up memories long forgotten; and who among us has not had memory triggered by the smell of pine needles scenting the air, the odor of burning leaves in fall, the fragrance of orange blossoms, eucalyptus, lilac or honeysuckle in spring? Helen Keller, discussing the potency of smell, once spoke of how it can transport us across thousands of miles and back many years. For her, fruit odors took her in an instant back to her Southern home and the peach orchard there.

Somewhere in our emergence from childhood we begin to realize that a tree is far more than its dictionary definition: "a woody perennial plant with one main stem or trunk ... commonly exceeding ten feet in height." It dawns upon us that a tree is one of the great natural gifts given to man by his Creator, that trees have long inspired the souls of poets and writers, that in woodlands man has found spiritual renewal to reknit nerves unraveled by the pressures of society. We realize in that moment of new awareness that we are indebted to trees not only for their contribution to the beauty of our world but for their great contribution to our comfort and well-being — for the homes we live in, the chairs we sit upon, the pencils we write with, the books we read.

There are over seven hundred species of trees. We hope that in the selection in this chapter you will find several that are familiar to you and perhaps some unfamiliar ones also, trees which you will enjoy looking for on your next hike in the country or on your next vacation in another part of the land. Leaf drawings and data have been included to aid you in recognizing these trees. When awareness is heightened, excursions into the country often include a series of small delights in the new found pleasure of recognition.

Young hard maple in autumn foliage, Hainesville, New Jersey.

Milwaukee County Park Commission

Dormant green ash tree in Wisconsin.

94

Leaf Color Change

All during spring and summer the leaves have served as factories where most of the foods necessary for the trees' growth are manufactured. This food-making process takes place in the leaf in numerous cells containing the pigment chlorophyll, which gives the leaf its green color. This chlorophyll absorbs energy from sunlight and uses it in transforming carbon dioxide and water to carbohydrates, such as sugars and starch. Along with the green pigment leaves also contain yellow or orange carotenoids — which, for example, give the carrot its familiar color. Most of the year these yellowish colors are masked by the greater amount of green coloring. But in the fall, partly because of changes in the period of daylight and changes in temperature, the leaves stop their food-making process. The chlorophyll breaks down, the green color disappears, and the yellowish colors become visible and give the leaves part of their fall splendor.

At the same time other chemical changes may occur and cause the formation of additional pigments that vary from yellow to red to blue. Some of them give rise to the reddish and purplish fall colors of leaves of trees such as dogwoods and sumacs. Others give the sugar maple its brilliant orange or fiery red and yellow. The autumn foliage of some trees, such as quaking aspen, birch and hickory, shows only yellow colors. Many oaks and others are mostly brownish, while beech turns golden bronze. These colors are due to the mixing of varying amounts of the chlorophyll and other pigments in the leaf during the fall season.

Fall weather conditions favoring formation of brilliant red autumn color are warm sunny days followed by cool nights with temperatures below 45 degrees F. Much sugar is made in the leaves during the daytime, but cool nights prevent movement of sugar from the leaves. From the sugars trapped in the leaves the red pigment called anthocyanin is formed. Familiar trees with red or scarlet leaves in autumn are red maple, silver maple, flowering dogwood, sweetgum, black tupelo or blackgum, Northern red oak, scarlet oak and sassafras.

The degree of color may vary from tree to tree. For example, leaves directly exposed to the sun may turn red, while those on the shady side of the same tree or on other trees in the shade may be yellow. The foliage of some tree species just turns dull brown from death and decay and never shows bright colors.

Also, the colors on the same tree may vary from year to year, depending upon the combination of weather conditions. When there is much warm, cloudy, rainy weather in the fall, the leaves may have less red coloration. The smaller amount of sugar made in the reduced sunlight moves out of the leaves during the warm nights. Thus, no excess sugar remains in the leaves to form the pigments.

Only a few regions of the world are fortunate in having these showy displays. Eastern United States possesses large areas of deciduous forests with broad-leaved trees and favorable weather conditions, including ample rainfall, for vivid fall colors. Some Western areas, especially in mountains, have bright coloration, too. The broad-leaved evergreen trees in the tropical rain forests shed their leaves very gradually, one at a time turning yellow and falling. In the seasonal tropical forests the foliage becomes parched and brown with the coming of the dry season.

As the fall colors appear, other changes are taking place. At the base of the leafstalk where it is attached to the twig, a special layer of cells develops and gradually severs the tissues that support the leaf. At the same time nature heals the break, so that after the leaf is finally blown off by the wind or has fallen from its own weight, the place where it grew on the twig is marked by a leaf scar.

Most broad-leaved trees in the North shed their leaves in the fall. However, the dead brown leaves of the oaks and a few other species may stay on the tree until growth starts again in the spring. In the South, where the winters are mild, some broad-leaved trees are evergreen; that is, the leaves stay on the trees during winter and keep their green color. Most conifers — pines, spruces, firs, hemlocks, cedars, etc. — are evergreen in both the North and South. The needlelike or scalelike leaves remain green or greenish the year round, though often becoming brownish green where winters are cold. Individual leaves may stay on the tree for two to four or more years.

Through fallen leaves, nature has provided for a fertile forest floor. Fallen leaves contain relatively large amounts of valuable elements, particularly calcium and potassium, which were originally a part of the soil. Decomposition of the leaves enriches the top layers of the soil by returning part of the elements borrowed by the tree, and at the same time provides for more water-absorbing humus.

... I discovered that she was looking eagerly at a tall ash tree that grew just inside the field fence.

"I thought 't was goin' to do well," she said complacently as we went on again. "Last time I was up this way that tree was kind of drooping and discouraged. Grown trees act that way sometimes, same's folks; then they'll put right to it and strike their roots off into new ground and start all over again with realgood courage. Ash trees is very likely to have poor spells; they ain't got the resolution of other trees."

....

"There's sometimes a good hearty tree growin' right out of the bare rock, out o' some crack that just holds the roots," she went on to say, "right on the pitch o' one o' them bare stony hills where you can't seem to see a wheel-barrowful o' good earth in a place, but that tree'll keep a green top in the driest summer. You lay your ear down to the ground an' you'll hear a little stream runnin'. Every such tree has got its own livin' spring; there's folks made to match 'em."

Sarah Orne Jewett
from *Country of the Pointed Firs*

This [paper birch] is the noblest of the birches, the white queen of the woods — the source of food, drink, transport and lodging to those who dwell in the forest; the most bountiful provider of all the trees.

Its sap yields a delicious syrup which has in it a healing balm for the lungs.

Its innermost bark is dried in famine time and powdered to a flour that has some nourishing power.

Its wood furnishes the rims for snowshoes, the frills and fuzzes of its outer bark are the best of fire kindlers, and the timber of the trunk has the rare property of burning whether green or dry.

Its catkins and buds form a favorite food of the partridge which is the choicest of game.

But the outer bark-skin, the famous birch bark, is its finest contribution to man's needs.

The broad sheets of this vegetable rawhide ripped off when the weather is warm and especially when the sap is moving — are tough, light, strong, pliant, absolutely waterproof, almost imperishable in the weather; free from insects, assailable only by fire. It roofs the settler's shack and the forest Indian wigwam, it is the "tin" of the woods and supplies pails, pots, pans, cups, spoons, boxes — under its protecting power the matches are safe and dry, and split very thin, as is easily done, it is the writing paper of the woods, flat, light, smooth, waterproof, tinted and scented; no daughter of the King has ever a more ex-

quisite sheet to sanctify the thoughts committed to its care.

But the crowning glory of the birch is this — it furnishes the indispensable substance for the bark canoe, whose making is the highest industrial exploit of the Indian life.

Ernest Thompson Seton

As I journey'd today in a light wagon ten or twelve miles through the country, nothing pleas'd me more, in their homely beauty and novelty (I had either never seen the little things to such advantage, or had never noticed them before) than that peculiar fruit, with its profuse clear-yellow dangles of inch-long silk or yarn, in boundless profusion spotting the dark green cedar bushes — contrasting well with their bronze tufts — the flossy shreds covering the knobs all over, like a shock of wild hair on elfin pates. On my ramble afterward down by the creek I pluck'd one from its bush, and shall keep it. These cedar-apples last only a little while however, and soon crumble and fade.

Walt Whitman
from *Specimen Days*

The orange, leading commercial fruit in the United States, was brought to these shores originally as a sour fruit by Spaniards who planted them in what is now Florida. The climate was excellent for the orange tree and it spread through the area, flourishing on drier knolls rising above generally marshy land. These sour oranges originally had been brought to Europe by merchant-traders returning from eastern India. Centuries later, around the beginning of the 1500's, Portuguese traders brought a sweet variety of orange from China and in the course of time these (and later other sweet varieties) were grafted onto the hardy, practically indigenous sour stock then growing in most parts of the state. From this beginning the citrus industry of Florida has developed into the most extensive of any state in the United States and is a key industry of that state.

The apple tree has been celebrated by the Hebrews, Greeks, Romans and Scandinavians. Some have thought that the first human pair were tempted by its fruit. Goddesses are fabled to have contended for it, dragons were set to watch it, and heroes were employed to pluck it.

The tree is mentioned in at least three places in the Old Testament, and its fruit in two or three more. Solomon sings, "As the apple-tree among the trees of the wood, so is my beloved among the sons," and "Stay me with flagons, comfort me with apples."

Henry David Thoreau

Aspens in high country of northern New Mexico.

96

Gene Ahrens

Cherry blossoms along Tidal Basin frame the Washington Monument.

Apple Tree

Apples have prospered in America for some three hundred years. It was about 1636 when Franciscan fathers planted an apple orchard at their mission in what is now New Mexico, near present day Manzano. The gnarled, old trees still grow in this orchard but the manner in which they are growing apparently indicates that the original crowns of these trees died and new shoots sprang up from the ancient, tenacious roots.

Even if I knew that tomorrow the
world would go to pieces,
I would still plant my apple tree.

Martin Luther

The remnant that is escaped .... shall again take root downward, and bear fruit upward.

— Isaiah 37:31

Young ginkgo tree.

Boerner Botanical Gardens, Milwaukee

Ancient Species

About halfway through the century of Christ's birth, cherry seeds accompanied Roman invasion forces entering England. In the years since cherries have reached every temperate corner of Europe and, of course, were brought from there to America. As with many of the fruit trees, the cherry came from Asia. The Romans got the cherry seeds from one of their generals, Lucullus, who in 70 B.C. returned to Rome with them from battles in distant lands.

Joshua trees near an atomic test site at the base of Nevada's Big Horn Mountains.

Perhaps the oldest of all extant tree species is the ginkgo, the only living species in its botanical order, the *Ginkgoales,* ancestors of which date back over 200 million years. Darwin termed this large ornamental tree with the unique fan-shaped leaves (also known as the maidenhair-tree) a "living fossil." It thrived 125 million years ago and its succulent leaves probably were part of the daily

The Joshua, a strange and ancient sort of tree whose ancestors first appeared about two million years ago, depends upon a symbiotic partnership with a small white moth for its survival. The Joshua produces large clusters of bell-shaped chartreuse-colored flowers in March and April. These flowers must be cross-pollinated by a carrier other than the wind since the Joshua's heavy petals do not spread outward as do others in the lily family, of which the Joshua is a member. And this is where the moth, *Pronuba,* comes into the picture.

Pronuba gathers pollen from the Joshua flower, rolls it into pellets and carries the pollen to another bloom, depositing the pelletized pollen deep in the blossom. A pod of seeds develops from each such fertilized blossom. Here the moth lays one egg. She repeats the process until she has laid each of her eggs in separate blossoms. The eggs, timed to hatch with the maturity of the seeds, allow the baby caterpillar to feed on the Joshua seeds. The partnership has been going on apparently since the Pliocene epoch because the Joshua's petrified wood tells bits of its story in stone.

———

By the sixth of October the leaves generally begin to fall, in successive showers, after frost or rain; but the principal leaf-harvest, the acme of the Fall, is commonly about the sixteenth. . . . When the morning wind rises, the leaves come down in denser showers than ever. They suddenly form thick beds or carpets on the ground. . . .

Henry David Thoreau
"Autumnal Tints"
from *Excursions*

fare of Brontosaurus dinosaur and other herbivores of the Jurassic period. It apparently disappeared during the ice age, but later reappeared under care in the remote, milder climate of interior China where ice-age destruction had been comparatively minor. The ginkgo has been propagated and protected for hundreds of centuries in Chinese and Japanese Buddhist and Taoist temple gardens and has been honored by cultivation in Lamaseries of Tibet. It is now common in Japan.

But think not that the splendor of the year is over; for as one leaf does not make a summer, neither does one falling leaf make an autumn. The smallest sugar maples in our streets make a great show as early as the fifth of October, more than any other trees there. As I look up the Main Street, they appear like painted screens standing before the houses. . . . They are remarkable for the contrast they often afford of deep blushing red on one half and green on the other. They become at length dense masses of rich yellow with a deep scarlet blush. . . . All the sunny warmth of the season, the Indian summer, seems to be absorbed in their leaves.

Henry David Thoreau
"Autumnal Tints"
from *Excursions*

Joseph Muench

Wind-shaped specimen of a coastal live oak in California.

Never was a tree more appropriately named than the red maple. Its first blossom flushes red in the April sunlight, its keys ripen scarlet in early May, all summer long its leaves swing on crimson or scarlet stems, its young twigs flame in the same colors and later, amid all the brilliancy of the autumnal forest, it stands preëminent and unapproachable.

Harriet Louise Keeler

Belonging to a genus which is remarkable for the beautiful form of its leaves, I suspect that some scarlet-oak leaves surpass those of all other oaks in the rich and wild beauty of their outlines.

Henry David Thoreau
"Autumnal Tints"
from *Excursions*

*Aspen and maple in early autumn,
Cache County, Utah.*

The actual objects which one man will see from a particular hill-top are just as different from those which another will see as the beholders are different. The scarlet oak must, in a sense, be in your eye when you go forth. We cannot see anything until we are possessed with the idea of it, take it into our heads, — and then we can hardly see anything else.

Henry David Thoreau
"Autumnal Tints"
from *Excursions*

Tulip tree *(Liriodendron)* is of the magnolia family — I have seen it in Michigan and southern Illinois, 140 feet high and 8 feet thick at the butt; does not transplant well; best rais'd from seeds — the lumbermen call it yellow poplar.

Walt Whitman
from *Specimen Days*

There are some grounds for connecting Brigit, like Vesta, with the oak; for at Kildare her Christian namesake, St. Brigit, otherwise known as St. Bride or St. Bridget, built her church under an oak tree, which existed till the tenth century, and gave its name to the spot, for Kildare is *Cilldara*, "the church of the oak tree." The "church of the oak" may well have displaced a temple or sanctuary of the oak, where in Druidical days the holy fire was fed, like the Vestal fire at Rome, with the wood of the sacred tree.

We may suspect that a conversion of this sort was often effected in Ireland by the early Christian missionaries. The monasteries of Derry and Durrow, founded by St. Columba, were both named after the oak groves amidst which they were built; and at Derry the saint spared the beautiful trees and strictly enjoined his successors to do the same. In his old age, when he lived an exile on the shores of the bleak storm-swept isle of Iona, his heart yearned to the home of his youth among the oak groves of Ireland, and he gave expression to the yearning in passionate verse: —

The dearest of any on Erin's ground,
For its peace and its beauty I gave it my
love;
Each leaf of the oaks around Derry is found
To be crowded with angels from heaven
above.

My Derry! my Derry! my little oak grove,
My dwelling, my home, and my own little
cell,
May God the Eternal in Heaven above
Send death to thy foes, and defend thee well.

Sir James G. Frazer
from *The Golden Bough*

June 2 — This is the fourth day of a dark northeast storm, wind and rain. Day before yesterday was my birthday. I have now enter'd on my 60th year. Every day of the storm, protected by overshoes and a waterproof blanket, I regularly come down to the pond, and ensconce myself under the lee of the great oak; I am here now writing these lines. . . .The soft green leaves dangle all around me. Seated here in solitude I have been musing over my life — connecting events, dates, as links of a chain, neither sadly nor cheerily, but somehow, today here under the oak, in the rain, in an unusually matter-of-fact spirit.

But my great oak—sturdy, vital, green—five feet thick at the butt. I sit a great deal near or under him. Then the tulip tree near by — the Apollo of the woods — tall and graceful, yet robust and sinewy, inimitable in hang of foliage and throwing-out of limb; as if the beauteous, vital, leafy creature could walk, if it only would.

Walt Whitman
from *Specimen Days*

The scarlet oak asks a clear sky and the brightness of late October days. These bring out its colors. If the sun goes into a cloud they become comparatively indistinct. As I sit on a cliff in the southwest part of our town, the sun is now getting low, and the woods in Lincoln, south and east of me, are lit up by its more level rays; and in the scarlet oaks, scattered so equally over the forest, there is brought out a more brilliant redness than I had believed was in them. Every tree of this species which is visible in those directions, even to the horizon, now stands out distinctly red. Some great ones lift their red backs high above the woods, in the next town, like huge roses with a myriad of fine petals; and some more slender ones, in a small grove of white pines on Pine Hill in the east, on the very verge of the horizon, alternating with the pines on the edge of the grove, and shouldering them with their red coats, look like soldiers in red amid hunters in green. This time it is Lincoln green, too. Till the sun got low, I did not believe that there were so many red coats in the forest army. Theirs is an intense burning red, which would lose some of its strength, methinks, with every step you might take toward them; for the shade that lurks amid their foliage does not report itself at this distance, and they are unanimously red. The focus of their reflected color is in the atmosphere far on this side. Every such tree becomes a nucleus of red, as it were, where, with the declining sun, that color grows and glows. It is partly borrowed fire, gathering strength from the sun on its way to your eye.

Henry David Thoreau
from *Excursions*

Out walking in the frozen swamp one grey day
I paused and said, "I will turn back from here.
No, I will go on farther — and we shall see."
The hard snow held me, save where now and
then
One foot went down. The view was all in lines
Straight up and down of tall slim trees
Too much alike to mark or name a place
by
So as to say for certain I was here
Or somewhere else: I was just far from home.
A small bird flew before me. He was careful
To put a tree between us when he lighted,

(continued on p.107)

The photographer's snowshoes rest against a Paul Bunyan-sized white pine in Sawyer County, Wisconsin.

Wind-blown white pine, Terry Andrae State Park, Wisconsin.

And say no word to tell me who he was
Who was so foolish as to think what *he*
    thought.
He thought that I was after him for a feather —
The white one in his tail; like one who takes
Everything said as personal to himself.
One flight out sideways would have
    undeceived him.
And then there was a pile of wood for which
I forgot him and let his little fear
Carry him off the way I might have gone,
Without so much as wishing him good-night.
He went behind it to make his last stand.
It was a cord of maple, cut and split
And piled — and measured, four by four by
    eight.
And not another like it could I see.
No runner tracks in this year's snow looped
    near it.
And it was older sure than this year's cutting,
Or even last year's or the year's before.

The wood was grey and the bark warping off it
And the pile somewhat sunken. Clematis
Had wound strings round and round it like a
    bundle.
What held it though on one side was a tree
Still growing, and on one a stake and prop,
These latter about to fall. I thought that only
Someone who lived in turning to fresh tasks
Could so forget his handiwork on which
He spent himself, the labour of his axe,
And leave it there far from a useful fireplace
To warm the frozen swamp as best it could
With the slow smokeless burning of decay.

Robert Frost
"The Wood-Pile"

Overleaf: *Ponderosa pine forest in
Los Padres National Forest on the flanks
of southern California's coastal mountains.*

*Ponderosa pine and small aspen grove
in Jemez Mountains of New Mexico.*

107

Thin lifelines of bark cling tenaciously to gnarled bristlecone pine, the earth's oldest single life.

Strange that so few ever come to the woods to see how the pine lives and grows and spires, lifting its evergreen arms to the light, — to see its perfect success. . . .

Henry David Thoreau
from *The Maine Woods*

The almost naked bristlecone pine (above) in the Patriarch Grove of California's White Mountains has endured for over four thousand years. Gnarled ancient roots (left) near Mount Washington, Oregon.

111

W. J. Weber

Young hemlock in an ancient coniferous forest.

The sycamore or plane tree, seen here in early winter, adapts readily to an urban environment.

The chestnut's proud and the lilac's pretty.
  The poplar's gentle and tall,
But the plane tree's kind to the poor dull
    city —
  I love him best of all!

>   Edith Nesbit
>   "Child's Song in Spring"

I think the hemlock likes to stand
Upon a marge of snow;
It suits his own austerity,
And satisfies an awe

That men must slake in wilderness,
Or in the desert cloy, —
An instinct for the hoar, the bald,
Lapland's necessity.

The hemlock's nature thrives on cold;
The gnash of northern winds
Is sweetest nutriment to him,
His best Norwegian wines.

To satin races he is nought;
But children on the Don
Beneath his tabernacles play,
And Dnieper wrestlers run.

>   Emily Dickinson

How the old mountains drip with sunset,
  And the brake of dun!
How the hemlocks are tipped in tinsel
  By the wizard sun!

>   Emily Dickinson

Blossoms of the tulip tree, or yellow poplar.

There is a tulip poplar within sight of Woodstown, which is twenty feet around, three feet from the ground, four feet across about eighteen feet up the trunk, which is broken off about three or four feet higher up. On the south side an arm has shot out from which rise two stems, each to about ninety-one or ninety-two feet from the ground. Twenty-five (or more) years since the cavity in the butt was large enough for, and nine men at one time, ate dinner therein. It is supposed twelve to fifteen men could now, at one time, stand within its trunk. The severe winds of 1877 and 1878 did not seem to damage it, and the two stems send out yearly many blossoms, scenting the air immediately about it with their sweet perfume. It is entirely unprotected by other trees, on a hill. — *Woodstown, N.J., "Register," April 15, '79.*

Walt Whitman
from *Specimen Days*

For many years the "oldest living tree" title went to the giant sequoias of California, but currently this honor belongs to the bristlecone pine. One of these trees has an authenticated age of over 4,600 years. Ancient Egypt was just emerging from its pre-dynastic period when this tree started to grow; the mists of some two thousand years lay between the tree's inception and the Golden Age of Pericles in Hellenic Greece; the Roman Empire established by Augustus in 27 B.C. was exactly 2,600 years in the future. Now the U.S. Forest Service has classified a 28,000-acre section of the Inyo National Forest in California near the Nevada border as "Ancient Bristlecone Pine Forest." Second and third runners-up are the massive big trees (*Sequoia gigantea*) and the redwoods (*S. sempervirens*) trailing 1,400 and 2,300 years behind the bristlecone.

Centuries of fallen needles make silence of my step, and the command upon the air, very soft, eternal, is to be still. I am at the knees of gods. I believe because I see, and to believe in these unimaginable titans strengthens the heart. Five thousand years of living, twelve

A sequoia tree is surrounded by Engelmann spruce. Mossy staghorn lichen protrude from spruce boles.

Big trees (Sequoia gigantea) *next to man-shaped pond, California.*

million pounds of growth out of a tiny seed. Three hundred vertical feet of growth, up which the water travels every day dead against gravity from deep in the great root system. Every ounce, every inch, was built upward from the earth by the thin invisible stream of protoplasm that has been handed down by the touch of pollen from generation to generation, for a hundred million years. Ancestral sequoias grew here before the Sierra was uplifted. Today they look down upon the plains of men. No one has ever known a sequoia to die a natural death. Neither insects nor fungi can corrupt them. Lightning may smite them at the crown and break it; no fire gets to the heart of them. They simply have no old age, and the only down trees are felled trees.

Donald Culross Peattie
from "The Sequoia"

The Big Tree keeps its youth far longer than any of its neighbors. Most silver firs are old in their second or third century, pines in their fourth or fifth, while the Big Tree growing beside them is still in the bloom of its youth, juvenile in every feature at the age of old pines, and cannot be said to attain anything like prime size and beauty before its fifteen hundredth year, or under favorable circumstances become old before its three thousandth. Many, no doubt, are much older than this. On one of the King's River giants, thirty-five feet and eight inches in diameter exclusive of bark, I counted upwards of four thousand annual wood rings, in which there was no trace of decay after all these centuries of mountain weather. There is no absolute limit to the existence of any tree. Their death is due to accidents, not, as of animals, to the wearing out of organs. Only the leaves die of old age, their fall is foretold in their structure; but the leaves are renewed every year and so also are the other essential organs — wood, roots, bark, buds. Most of the Sierra trees die of disease. Thus the magnificent silver firs are devoured by fungi, and comparatively few of them live to see their three hundredth birth year. But nothing hurts the Big Tree. I never saw one that was sick or showed the slightest sign of decay. It lives on through indefinite

Giant sequoias at seven thousand feet in the Sierra Nevadas of California.

Ed Weber

Gene Ahrens

Avenue of the Giants, Humboldt Redwoods State Park, California.

thousands of years until burned, blown down, undermined, or shattered by some tremendous lightning stroke. No ordinary bolt ever seriously hurts sequoia. In all my walks I have seen only one that was thus killed outright.

I have seen silver firs two hundred feet high split into long peeled rails and slivers down to the roots, leaving not even a stump, the rails radiating like the spokes of a wheel from a hole in the ground where the tree stood. But the sequoia, instead of being split and slivered, usually has forty or fifty feet of its brash, knotty top smashed off in short chunks about the size of cord-wood, the beautiful rosy red ruins covering the ground in a circle.

It is a curious fact that all the very old sequoias have lost their heads by lightning. "All things come to him who waits." But of all living things sequoia is perhaps the only one able to wait long enough to make sure of being struck by lightning. Thousands of years it stands ready and waiting, offering its head to every passing cloud as if inviting its fate, praying for heaven's fire as a blessing; and when at last the old head is off, another of the same shape immediately begins to grow on. Every bud and branch seems excited, like bees that have lost their queen, and tries hard to repair the damage. Branches that for many centuries have been growing out horizontally at once turn upward and all their branchlets arrange themselves with reference to a new top of the same peculiar curve as the old one.

Even the small subordinate branches halfway down the trunk do their best to push up to the top and help in this curious head-making.

John Muir
from "The Sequoia"

A prophecy and indirection, a thought
    impalpable to breathe as air,
A chorus of dryads, fading, departing, or
    hamadryads departing,
A murmuring, fateful, giant voice, out of the
    earth and sky,
Voice of a mighty dying tree in the redwood
    forest dense.

Farewell my brethren,
Farewell O earth and sky, farewell ye
    neighboring waters,
My time has ended, my term has come.

Along the northern coast,
Just back from the rock-bound shore and the
    caves,
In the saline air from the sea in the Mendocino
    country,
With the surge for base and accompaniment
    low and hoarse,
With crackling blows of axes sounding
    musically driven by strong arms,
Riven deep by the sharp tongues of the axes,
    there in the redwood forest dense,
I heard the mighty tree its death-chant
    chanting.
The choppers heard not, the camp shanties
    echoed not,

The quick-ear'd teamsters and chain and jack-
    screw men heard not,
As the wood-spirits came from their haunts of
    a thousand years to join the refrain,
But in my soul I plainly heard.
Murmuring out of its myriad leaves,
Down from its lofty top rising two hundred feet
    high,
Out of its stalwart trunk and limbs, out of its
    foot-thick bark,
That chant of the seasons and time, chant not
    of the past only but the future.

You untold life of me,
And all you venerable and innocent joys,
Perennial hardy life of me with joys 'mid rain
    and many a summer sun,
And the white snows and night and the wild
    winds;
O the great patient rugged joys, my soul'd
    strong joys unreck'd by man,
(For know I bear the soul befitting me, I too
    have consciousness, identity,
And all the rocks and mountains have, and all
    the earth,)
Joys of the life befitting me and brothers
    mine,
Our time, our term has come.

Nor yield we mournfully majestic brothers,
We who have grandly fill'd our time;
With Nature's calm content, with tacit huge
    delight,
We welcome what we wrought for through the
    past,
And leave the field for them.
For them predicted long,
For a superber race, they too to grandly fill
    their time,
For them we abdicate, in them ourselves ye
    forest kings!
In them these skies and airs, these mountain
    peaks, Shasta, Nevadas,
These huge precipitous cliffs, this amplitude,
    these valleys, far Yosemite,
To be in them absorb'd assimilated.

Then to a loftier strain,
Still prouder, more ecstatic rose the chant,
As if the heirs, the deities of the West,
Joining with master-tongue bore part.

Not wan from Asia's fetiches,
Nor red from Europe's old dynastic slaughter-
    house,
(Area of murder-plots of thrones, with scent
    left yet of wars and scaffolds everywhere,)
But come from Nature's long and harmless
    throes, peacefully builded thence,
These virgin lands, lands of the Western shore,
To the new culminating man, to you, the
    empire new,
You promis'd long, we pledge, we dedicate.

You occult deep volitions,
You average spiritual manhood, purpose of
    all, pois'd on yourself, giving not taking
    law.
You womanhood divine, mistress and source
    of all, whence life and love and aught that
    comes from life and love,
You unseen moral essence of all the vast
    materials of America, (age upon age
    working in death the same as life,)
You that, sometimes known, oftener unknown,
    really shape and mould the New World,
    adjusting it to Time and Space,
You hidden national will lying in your
    abysms, conceal'd but ever alert,
You past and present purposes tenaciously
    pursued, may-be unconscious of
    yourselves,
Unswerv'd by all the passing errors,
    perturbations of the surface;
You vital, universal, deathless germs, beneath
    all creeds, arts, statutes, literatures,
Here build your homes for good, establish
    here, these areas entire, lands of the
    Western shore,
We pledge, we dedicate to you.

For man of you, your characteristic race,
Here may he hardy, sweet, gigantic grow,
    here tower proportionate to Nature,
Here climb the vast pure spaces unconfined,
    uncheck'd by wall or roof,
Here laugh with storm or sun, here joy, here
    patiently inure,
Here heed himself, unfold himself, (not others'
    formulas heed,) here fill his time,
To duty fall, to aid, unreck'd at last,
To disappear, to serve.

Thus on the northern coast,
In the echo of teamsters' calls and the clinking
    chains, and the music of choppers' axes,
The falling trunk and limbs, the crash, the
    muffled shriek, the groan,
Such words combined from the redwood-tree,
    as of voices ecstatic, ancient and rustling,
The century-lasting, unseen dryads, singing,
    withdrawing,
All their recesses of forests and mountains
    leaving,
From the Cascade range to the Wasatch, or
    Idaho far, or Utah,
To the deities of the modern henceforth
    yielding,
The chorus and indications, the vistas of
    coming humanity, the settlements,
    features all
In the Mendocino woods I caught.

Walt Whitman
"Song of the Redwood Tree"

Overleaf: *Scarlet, rust and gold*
        . . . leaves and needles.
Tom Algire

BRIEF GUIDE TO COMMON SPECIES

I Gymnosperms

PINE FAMILY (Conifers)
pine-larch-spruce-fir-hemlock-
sequoia-cypress-cedar-juniper

YEW FAMILY
yew

GINKGO FAMILY
ginkgo

II Angiosperms

LILY FAMILY
palmetto-yucca (Joshua tree)

WILLOW FAMILY
willow-aspen-cottonwood

WALNUT FAMILY
walnut-hickory-pecan

BIRCH FAMILY
birch-alder-hophornbeam

BEECH FAMILY
beech-chestnut-oak

ELM FAMILY
elm-hackberry

MULBERRY FAMILY
mulberry

MAGNOLIA FAMILY
tulip tree-magnolia

LAUREL FAMILY
sassafras

WITCH HAZEL FAMILY
sweetgum

PLANETREE FAMILY
sycamore

ROSE FAMILY
black cherry

PULSE FAMILY
locust

MAPLE FAMILY
maple-box elder

HORSECHESTNUT (BUCKEYE) FAMILY
horsechestnut

LINDEN FAMILY
basswood

CACTUS FAMILY
saguaro

DOGWOOD FAMILY
dogwood

OLIVE FAMILY
ash

BIGNONIA FAMILY
catalpa

EASTERN WHITE PINE

(Pinus strobus)
80' to 125' tall — 2' to 5' diameter

LEAVES The needles of the Eastern white pine distinguish it from all the other eastern pines by the fact that the three- to five-inch needles occur in bundles of five. The needles are bluish green above, whitish green beneath.

FLOWERS Female flowers appear several years before the male are produced. The female strobils are usually in the upper portion of the tree crown, the male clustered in the lower branches.

FRUIT The cylindrical cones are three to five inches long, have thin, usually very gummy scales containing small (one-fourth inch) winged seeds.

BARK Smooth, greenish bark characterizes the young white pine; on older trees it becomes rugged: thick, strongly ridged, deeply furrowed and dark gray-brown in color.

LONGLEAF PINE

(Pinus palustris)
80' to 100' tall — 1-1/2' to 2-1/2'
diameter

LEAVES   The needles of the longleaf are possibly the longest of any pine, from about eight to eighteen inches. The bundles of three are contained in dense tufts at the tips of twigs and branches. The flexible, slender needles droop slightly. Their color is a lustrous light yellowish green.

FRUIT   The six- to ten-inch cones, curved a little, are the longest of any of the Southern pines and have scales that are flat and thin with a small prickle at the rounded end.

BARK   The thin (one-sixth to one-half inch) light yellowish-brown bark is irregularly marked by narrow fissures and sometimes becomes partly detached at the fissure line, giving the bark a moderately scaly appearance.

Photograph on page 69

LODGEPOLE PINE

(Pinus contorta)
75' to 80' tall — 1' to 3' diameter

NEEDLES   Two lodgepole needles are bound at the base in pairs, are stiff, slightly curved, about two inches long and bright yellow-green.

FRUIT   The lodgepole pine might be called a phoenix tree since it reseeds very easily in burned-over areas. The reason for this is that the cone remains tightly closed until it is heated, when it readily opens. The pale brown asymmetrical cones are one to two inches long and the tight, hard scales have a small, curving prickle.

BARK   The bark is moderately rough and ridged, gray-brown, with small scales about two inches square and is an inch thick or less.

RED PINE

(Pinus resinosa)
70' to 90' tall — 2' to 3' diameter

NEEDLES   Shiny, five-inch, medium green needles grow in clusters of two, encased by a small sheath at the base of the bundle where it joins the branch. The slender flexible needles fall off in their fourth or fifth year.

CONES   The egg-shaped cones grow to a length of about two inches and are light red-brown in color.

BARK   The bark of the mature trunk is scaly with a distinctly red-brown color. On new growth, the bark is yellowish, changing as it matures.

SHORTLEAF PINE

NEEDLES The soft needles, or "straw," are mostly in clusters of two or three, are dark bluish green in color and from two to five inches in length.

FRUIT The abundant cones of echinata grow in opposed pairs at right angles from the branch and are among the smallest of pine cones in length. In shape they resemble a small pullet egg. Cone scales are each tipped by a fine needle-pointed prickle.

BARK The bark is pale reddish brown and coarsely fissured.

OTHER FEATURES In common with loblolly, longleaf and slash, shortleaf pine is also called "yellow pine" or "Southern yellow pine."

Shortleaf pine can readily reproduce itself and has the ability to sprout after fire or cutting. Few other important U.S. pines reproduce as prolifically.

(Pinus echinata)
70' to 100' tall — 1' to 3' diameter

SUGAR PINE

NEEDLES The needles of the tallest of all the pines grow in bundles of five and are two and a half to four inches long. They have the deep blue-green and whitish tinge typical of true white pines and are stout, stiff and twisted, remaining on the twig through their third year.

FRUIT The cones, light green or pale purple when young, become dark purple-brown before maturing and stand erect on the twig, giving the tree the name "purple-coned sugar pine." They are the largest of all pine cones, maturing at ten to twenty inches.

BARK The bark is thin, smooth and dull dark green-gray. Mature sugar pine tree bark is two or three inches thick, deeply grooved and reddish brown in color.

"The largest, noblest, and most beautiful of all 70 or 80 species of pine in the world."

John Muir

(Pinus lambertiana)
160' to 210' tall — 2' to 6' diameter

SCOTCH PINE

(Pinus sylvestris)
(Not Native)
35' to 50' tall — 10" to 20" diameter

NEEDLES Inflexible one- to three-inch yellow-green needles grow in bunches of two, encased by a sheath at the base.

CONES The egg-shaped, finger length cones have tightly clustered, prickle-tipped scales on their lower third to half, but are more diffuse in the upper portion.

BARK Ridged and furrowed red-brown bark on older trees develops from the scaly rusty orange of younger trees.

BRISTLECONE PINE

(Pinus aristata)
20' to 50' tall — 1' to 3' diameter

NEEDLES Bushy growth of one- to one-and-a-half-inch needles which remain on the tree for a dozen or more years denotes the bristlecone pine.

FLOWERS In color, the pistillate flowers are deep purple and the staminate a deep orange-red.

CONE Quarter-inch-long slender but stiff prickles, bent in like the fingers of a requesting, outstretched hand, are at the end of each scale of each three-inch cone and give the bristlecone its name.

BARK The half- to three-quarter-inch-thick bark, where it is found on these frequently ancient trees, ranges from pale white on younger trees to reddish brown as the tree ages.

The bristlecone pine is believed to be the oldest living thing on earth. A California specimen is 4,600 years old.

Photograph on page 110

PONDEROSA PINE

NEEDLES Ponderosa needles are a deep yellow-green, five to sometimes ten inches long, three needles to a bunch bound at the base either growing in clusters or scattered along the stems, the outer limbs giving an impression of bristly fox tails.

FRUIT The young cones are erect, tight and bright green. As the cones mature they turn brown or reddish brown, the scales open and the cones droop. There is a small sharp prickle on the hard cone scales.

BARK Bark on the young trees is black and crinkled, becoming cinnamon-brown and then, approaching maturity, blocks of orange-yellow plates with irregular fissures an inch or two deep develop. A noticeable turpentine odor emanates from the bark.

Photograph on page 108

(Pinus ponderosa)
150' to 230' tall — 3' to 7' diameter

TAMARACK, LARCH

NEEDLES Soft, triangular needles have a keel-like ridge on the lower side, are three-quarters to an inch and a quarter long and grow in clusters or rosettes. These green needles turn golden yellow in the autumn and fall off leaving a hump on the twig.

BARK The soft red-brown bark, one-half to three-quarters of an inch thick, is separated into small scales.

FLOWERS The tamarack bears bright red pistillate flowers early in summer.

FRUIT The half-inch chestnut-brown cones are ovoid in shape.

(Larix laricina)
50' to 60' tall — 1' to 2' diameter

ENGELMANN SPRUCE

(Picea engelmannii)
90' to 120' tall—1-1/2' to 3' diameter

LEAVES Needles are straight, slender and flexible on some branches but shorter and stiffer on others, dark blue-green in color and marked by rows of stomata.

FLOWERS Staminate flowers are dark purple and the pistillate are a bright red. All of the foliage of this tree is malodorous.

FRUIT The pale green, sometimes red-tinged, two-inch cones grow profusely on the topmost branches of the Engelmann spruce and become a shiny, light red-brown in color before the seeds are released and the cones dropped.

BARK The half-inch-thick, burnt orange to red-brown bark is broken into thin, large scales.

Photograph on page 115

SITKA SPRUCE

(Picea sitchensis)
180' to 210' tall — 4' to 6' diameter

LEAVES The sharp-tipped leaves are slightly flattened, lustrous green and almost covered by white bands of numerous rows of stomata on the upper surface. They project from all of the surface of twig or branch, usually at nearly a right angle.

FLOWERS The dark red, staminate, pollen-bearing flowers grow at the ends of drooping branchlets. The pistillate, seed-producing flowers form on rigid terminal shoots of the branches on the top half of the tree.

FRUIT Sitka cones — oblong and two to four inches long — grow on a short stalk and are pale yellow with a deep red or red-brown cast when mature. The cones carry round one-eighth-inch seeds with wings, a fifth of a million to a pound.

BARK Sitka bark is thin and broken into deep auburn colored scales loosely connected to the tree.

DOUGLAS FIR

(Pseudotsuga menziesii)
100' to 300' tall — 2' to 10' diameter

NEEDLES The needles, about one inch long, grow directly from the twig and protrude all around it giving a fingerlike shape to each twig. Needles are firm but not stiff, with blunt ends, and exude a rich "piney" odor. A small stem (petiole) at the base of the flat, slightly grooved-on-top needle helps distinguish the Douglas fir from a true fir, such as the balsam.

FRUIT The two- to three-inch-long, two-inch-thick reddish-brown cones are pendant. Distinctive three-pronged bracts protruding from among the cone scales are longer than the scales.

BARK In mature trees the hard, tough corky bark is gray with a red-brown cast and is six inches to more than a foot thick with deep fissures.

CLASSIFICATION *Pseudotsuga* means "false hemlock." *Menziesii* is a species name given by botanists (after Archibald Menzies, who first saw and described the tree in 1792) to replace "taxifolia," i.e., "with leaves like the yew." In fact, the tree is neither pine nor spruce nor hemlock nor yew; it is not even fir. It is in a family almost entirely to itself. Its only other family member is Bigcone Douglas fir *(Pseudotsuga macrocarpa)*.

Photograph on page 163

SUBALPINE FIR

(Abies lasiocarpa)
60' to 90' tall — 14" to 24" diameter

LEAVES The "alpine" fir needles are deep blue-green in color with a silvery tinge on new growth each year. The flat, blunt-ended needles are an inch to inch and a half long on lower branches, but are pointed and seldom over half an inch on upper branches.

FLOWERS Staminate and pistillate flowers are found only on the upper half of the tree, the staminate being in color a deep indigo blue but becoming violet when the flower opens (and shortly before). The color of the pistillate flower is dark violet-purple.

FRUIT Deep purple is also the color of the two- to four-inch-long cone. The cones, which stand upright on the branches, turn a lighter shade of purple by the time the scales fall.

BARK The ash-gray or white bark of the subalpine fir is smooth and hard but, as in all balsam firs, is marked by blisterlike resin pockets. Old trees have pale brown seams and cracks, particularly near the base.

Photograph on page 64

WHITE FIR

(Abies concolor)
150' to 200' tall — 2' to 5' diameter

NEEDLES The narrow, flat, usually rounded-tip needles are conspicuous for different lengths — one to three inches — on the same twig, often with the long needles toward twig end. They are pale yellow-green with a distinct whitish cast.

FRUIT The tight-scaled, pale green or yellow and purplish-green three- to five-inch cones grow upright at the end of branches. They are sometimes hard to find, falling apart when ripe.

BARK Young bark is generally smooth but spotted with balsam blisters and is a slightly mottled white-gray color. Older bark might be six inches thick and has become rough and hard with ridges and furrows, but retains the mottled white-gray color.

BALSAM FIR

(Abies balsamea)
40' to 60' tall — 1' to 1-1/2' diameter

NEEDLES Flat balsam needles curve outwards immediately from the branch. They grow to three-quarters to one-and-a-half-inch length in opposed pairs.

FRUIT The cones — oblong cylinders with rounded tips — are a dark, rich purple and are two to four inches long. They grow upright from the branch and disintegrate on maturity.

BARK Mature tree bark is a rich red-brown color, broken into small plates with scales. Resin blisters dot the bark of young balsams.

129

EASTERN HEMLOCK

LEAVES The flat needles of the Eastern hemlock are about a half inch long and taper from the base to the apex. They are lustrous dark green in color. A double row of five or six white stomata dots are on the underside, while the upper side is slightly grooved. They fall from the tree in their third year, leaving an orange hued base.

FLOWERS Stamen of the Eastern hemlock are a light yellow while the pistils are a pale green. The broad leaves of the flowers are serrated on the edges and are shorter than the scales.

FRUIT The half-inch ovoid cones of the Eastern hemlock grow on quarter-inch stems. Each scale is broadly oval in shape.

BARK The cinammon-red to a gray bark of the Eastern hemlock has a purple tint. It is deeply divided into narrow, rounded ridges on mature trees. On younger trees the bark has more of a red-brown cast.

(Tsuga canadensis)
60' to 70' tall — 2' to 4' diameter

Photograph on page 112

REDWOOD

NEEDLES The dark green top, silver–green bottom needle always has a small prickle at the end of its irregular (one-fourth inch to one inch) length. Needles resemble flat awls and each twig bears fifty or more needles in a flat spray.

FRUIT The oblong cones, about an inch long and half as wide, ripen in October, bearing the light brown seeds about a sixteenth of an inch long which are capable of producing giants more than 350 feet tall. The dark brown cones grow at the ends of branchlets and their blunt-ended scales open to drop the wingless seeds.

BARK Redwood bark is eight to twelve inches thick, soft-appearing with irregular deep furrows and ridges up and down the trunk. Older trunks are very dark brown while younger trees have the red-brown bark that gave the tree its common name. A second, inner layer of bark is cinnamon-red color.

(Sequoia sempervirens)
200' to 350' tall — 10' to 15' diameter

Photograph on page 118

GIANT SEQUOIA

(Sequoia gigantea)
200' to 300' tall — 10' to 30' diameter
(This tree is also called big tree,
sequoia and Sierra redwood)

NEEDLES Needles are shaped like sharp awls or narrow lancelike wedges growing close against and completely around twigs and branchlets. Needles, seldom more than a quarter inch long, actually overlap somewhat like fish scales. Their color is deep blue-green, occasionally bright green.

FRUIT Cones are the size and shape of a pullet egg, two to three inches long and about an inch and a half to two and a half inches in diameter. The blunt-ended scales are olive green when young turning to dull brown as they mature. The seeds, about one-eighth inch long, are only slightly larger than those of *sempervirens*.

BARK Cinnamon-brown with a dull silver surface on older boles colors the soft, fibrous, deep vertically grooved bark. Bases of older trees, covered by one-to two-feet-thick bark, are heavily buttressed near the ground to help support the massive trunks. Diameters have exceeded thirty feet (see John Muir, page 116).

Photograph on page 31

BALDCYPRESS

(Taxodium distichum)
100' to 120' tall — 4' to 6' diameter

LEAVES The tiny (one-half to three-quarters inch) leaves of baldcypress are arranged in featherlike fashion along the sides of small branchlets. Light yellow-green in color, the leaf clusters resemble miniature fern fronds. In autumn the branchlets fall with the leaves still attached. This characteristic of leaf shedding is shared with only two other conifer genera — larch and metasequoia, the "dawn redwood" of China.

FLOWERS Baldcypress flowers blossom in spring and give the tree a delicate purple tinge.

FRUIT The fruit is a rounded cone or "ball" about a half inch to an inch in diameter often found in pairs at the end of a branch. The small enclosed seeds have wings about a quarter inch long.

BARK The light cinnamon-red bark is one to two inches thick and finely divided by numerous shallow, vertical fissures.

EASTERN RED CEDAR

LEAVES There are two kinds, both sometimes found on the same tree. The commoner kind is dark green, minute and scalelike, clasping the stem in four ranks, so that the stems appear square. Less common, often appearing on young growth or new shoots, is a kind that is awl-shaped, sharp-pointed, spreading and whitened beneath.

FLOWERS The two kinds of flowers, blossoming in February or March, are at the end of the twigs on separate trees. Staminate trees take on a golden color from the small catkins which, when shaken, shed clouds of yellow pollen.

FRUIT The fruit is a pale blue berry with a white bloom, a quarter inch in diameter, with sweet flesh that is a favorite winter food for birds.

BARK The bark is very thin, reddish brown, peeling off in long strips. The trunk of this irregular growing tree is often erratically grooved.

(Juniperus virginiana)
40' to 60' tall — 1' to 3' diameter

Photograph on page 81

NORTHERN WHITE CEDAR

NEEDLES Flattened scales growing alternately at right angles to one another, forming alternate pairs, distinguish the white cedar.

FRUIT The cones, up to a half inch long, ripen and release their small wing-bearing seeds in early October.

BARK The thin fibrous bark is fissured and in color is a light reddish brown.

(Thuja occidentalis)
50' to 60' tall — 2' to 3' diameter

INCENSE CEDAR

LEAVES The small leaves, resembling tiny fish scales, grow completely around the twigs and are one-eighth to half an inch long, with a slight prickle at the end. The pale yellow-green leaves overlap, with four around a twig stem. Twigs grow in flat sprays, resembling lacy fans, three to seven inches long.

FLOWERS Flowers appear in January, the tree taking on a golden cast from the myriad quarter-inch-long stamen.

FRUIT Mature cones three-quarters to one inch long droop at the end of a branch. They are light brown in color becoming red-brown, somewhat resembling a narrow acorn until they open, then the sides split and deliver the tiny (one-eighth inch) seed.

BARK Young, cinnamon reddish-brown bark is soft and tends to flake off in small plates. Mature bark is dark, rich red-brown with deep vertical furrows resembling the sequoia.

(Libocedrus decurrens)
80' to 110' tall — 3' to 5' diameter

CALIFORNIA JUNIPER

LEAVES A distinguishing feature of the California juniper are its leaves which grow in groups of three around the stem. Each leaf is about one-eighth inch long and grows tightly pressed to the branch. It has a waxy texture and is yellow-green in color. There is a distinct fringe on the margin.

FLOWERS The flowers appear from January to March. Stamens grow in groups of three to form staminates of eighteen to twenty-one members. The scales of the pistillate flower usually are six in number and are almost obliterated on the fruit.

FRUIT The red-brown fruit, the juniper berry, is globular in shape and about a half-inch long. It has a waxy skin, fibrous, dry flesh and one or two large seeds.

BARK The thin bark is ash-gray in color and is divided into long loose plate-like scales.

(Juniperus californica)
30' to 40' tall — 1' to 2' diameter

PACIFIC YEW

LEAVES The needles of the Pacific yew are one-half to three-fourths inch long and are a dark yellow-green above and paler below.

FLOWERS At the apex of a slender stalk is a globular head with four to eight pale yellow flowers with four to six cone-shaped pollen sacs hanging from each.

FRUIT The small, gray-green seed is surrounded by a sweet, juicy, scarlet disk.

BARK The quarter-inch-thick bark is reddish purple and scaly.

(Taxus brevifolia)
40' to 50' tall — 1' to 2-1/2' diameter

GINKGO

LEAVES The distinctive fan-shaped leaves with a notch opposite the stem mark the ginkgo, the last surviving species of a widespread group of trees 200,000,000 years ago. The *Ginkgo biloba* itself dates back 125 million years. The light green summer leaf turns to a bright yellow in autumn prior to the limited one or two day golden shower of virtually all the leaves from the tree. The leaf is about three inches wide and one and a half to two and a half long.

FRUIT The round, orange-yellow fruit is about an inch in diameter, contains a large white seed and gives off a foul odor as it disintegrates, the main reason why few pistillate trees are planted in cities, even though the tree is one of the most adaptable to usual city pollutants and contaminants.

BARK The bark of a young ginkgo is generally smooth and a light gray in color interrupted by light tan veins which develop into shallow fissures as the tree grows. When the tree is mature the fissures have widened to about one to four inches and have deepened to about half an inch to an inch and a half. The color of the mature tree is dark gray with red–brown tinges.

(Ginkgo biloba)
(Not Native)
Up to 100' tall — Up to 3' diameter

Photograph on page 99

CABBAGE PALMETTO

(Sabal palmetto)
30' to 40' tall — 1' to 2' diameter

LEAVES The leaves are from five to eight feet long and usually broader than long, dark green, shiny and the fan shape of the leaf is deeply divided into narrow blades and is carried on a stem five to seven feet long.

FLOWERS A fleshy two-inch spike carries numerous small clusters of red-flushed flowers that open in June.

FRUIT The fruit consists of rounded one-third–inch diameter berries, each containing a single quarter–inch, brown seed which ripens late in autumn.

WOOD The wood is light, soft, pale brown and contains many hard, fibrous threads; the outer rim is about two inches thick and is lighter and softer than the interior.

JOSHUA TREE

(Yucca brevifolia)
25' to 60' tall — 2' to 3' diameter

LEAVES Clusters of very thin, rapier-shaped leaves, about six to ten inches long grow from the ends of irregular, bulky, thickset branches.

FLOWERS One-to two-inch greenish-white flowers grow in clusters, eight to ten inches long.

FRUIT The fruit is an oblong pod, two to four inches long, two inches in diameter, yellow-brown in color and generally triangular in cross section.

BARK Deep divisions in the inch-and-a-half-thick bark form plates often a foot and a half to nearly double that in length.

Photograph on page 57

BLACK WILLOW

(Salix nigra)
30' to 40' tall — 1' to 3' diameter

LEAVES The alternate leaves of the black willow are bright, light lustrous green in color. Lanceolate in shape, they taper to a long curved tip. The base of the leave is rounded or wedge shaped. Generally smooth in texture, they have finely serrated edges.

FLOWERS The flowers of the black willow are bisexual spikes, one to three inches long. The short yellow scales are rounded at the apex and are coated on the inner surface with pale hairs.

FRUIT The smooth textured fruit of the black willow is somewhat conical in shape. It is about one-eighth inch long and light red-brown in color.

BARK The bark is dark brown or nearly black in color and is about an inch thick and is heavily ridged to form platelike scales. It has a shaggy appearance on mature trees.

QUAKING ASPEN

LEAVES The leaves are on slender, flat petioles, arranged alternately on the twigs, and are spade-shaped: broadly oval and short pointed. The edges are shallowly toothed. The leaf that trembles in the merest zephyr is a shiny green above and dull below.

FLOWERS Flowers are in catkins and appear before the leaves begin to expand. The two kinds are borne on separate trees; staminate catkins are about two inches long, but the seed producing flowers form a long slender cluster four inches in length.

FRUIT The fruit is a conical capsule filled with tiny cottony seeds which ripen in late spring before the leaves are fully expanded.

BARK The bark is thin, smooth and varies from cream-white to gray tinged with green.

Photograph on page 162

(Populus tremuloides)
20' to 40' tall — 10"to 20" diameter

EASTERN COTTONWOOD

LEAVES The simple, spade-shaped leaves have large single teeth around the serrated edges. Although the leaf is only three to six inches long it may be as wide as five inches across the flat base.

FLOWERS Staminate and pistillate catkins appear on separate trees before the leaves.

FRUIT The fruit ripens in late spring, appearing as long drooping strings of ovoid capsules filled with small seeds. These strings of fruit, each five to eight inches long, give to the tree the name "necklace poplar." The tiny seeds enclosed are covered with white cottony hair.

BARK The bark on young trees is light gray-green, sometimes with a tinge of yellow, becoming a wrinkled, ridged and grooved dark gray in maturity, about one to two inches thick.

(Populus deltoides)
60' to 90' tall — 5' to 7' diameter

136

BLACK WALNUT

LEAVES The opposite, odd-compound leaves are in a frondlike arrangement of fifteen to twenty-three yellowish-green leaflets paired along both sides of a leafstalk with a single one at the tip. The leaflets are about three inches long, sharply tapered at the end, about three-quarters of an inch to an inch across and are finely serrated along the margin.

FRUIT The nuts, borne singly or in pairs, are enclosed in a solid green husk which does not split open when the nut is ripe, like the hickory. This husk contains a very dark brown oil which stains the bare hands of anyone seeking the highly nutritious and edible nut inside. The nut is contained within a ridged, thick and very hard shell.

BARK The bark of the black walnut is divided into rounded ridges by the deep and rather narrow fissures between. It is thick and charcoal brown in color.

(Juglans nigra)
60' to 100' tall—1-1/2' to 3' diameter

SHAGBARK HICKORY

LEAVES Usually five, and infrequently seven or nine wide lanceolate leaflets make up the compound alternate leaf of the shagbark hickory. The compound leaf is seven to fourteen inches long.

FRUIT The nearly round shell is from one to two inches in diameter and splits open, when ripe, along four deeply grooved seams. The contained husk is often oval in horizontal plane, orbicular in vertical, pale whitish tan in color, usually with four prominent ridges and often with two to four additional obscure ridges. The husk is hard but the kernel or seed is sweet, aromatic and edible.

BARK The mature trees have a distinctive rough shaggy bark made up of narrow long plates or strips, curved away from the tree at the ends, often only slightly attached.

(Carya ovata)
70' to 90' tall — 1' to 2' diameter

PECAN

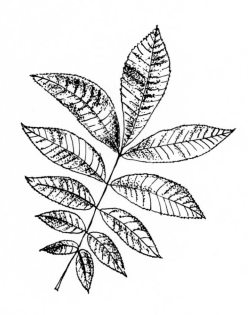

LEAVES The compound leaf of the pecan is twelve to twenty inches long and is composed of nine to seventeen lanceolate leaflets. These toothed leaflets are somewhat curved at their narrow tips. The dark, yellow-green surface of the leaf is smooth in texture. The paler underside may be slightly hairy in texture.

FLOWERS The yellow-green catkins are three to five inches long and grow in clusters near the ends of branches. The catkin flowers are hairy in texture with ovate lobes.

FRUIT The pecan nut grows in clusters of three to eleven. A hard, brittle, two-inch husk covers the nut. When ripe, the husk splits into four distinct parts. The nut is smooth in texture and ovoid to ellipsoid in shape and nearly cylindrical. The nut shell is paper thin and covers a sweet red-brown seed, which is formed into two nearly flat oblong lobes.

BARK The light brown bark is about an inch thick. The surface is marked with irregular furrowed forks and ridges.

(Carya illinoensis)
100' to 170' tall — 4' to 6' diameter

Photograph on page 84

PAPER BIRCH

LEAVES Paper birch leaves are spade shaped with either a rounded or occasionally cordate base and coarse, usually double-toothed serrated edges. They are dark green and are from two to three inches long and one to two inches wide.

FRUIT The staminate spikelike flower clusters of the birch are three to four inches long. The tubular strobiles disintegrate on maturity and scatter the one-sixteenth-inch seeds.

BARK Young birches have a red-brown bark, but as the tree matures it changes to a distinctive white, mottled with black. The paperlike bark peels into long strips, the joy of boys and the bane of foresters.

(Betula papyrifera)
60' to 70' tall — 1-1/2' to 3' diameter

YELLOW BIRCH

(Betula alleghaniensis)
60' to 80' tall — 1' to 3' diameter

LEAVES The egg-shaped, pointed-tip leaves are three to four inches long and often in pairs. They are dull dark green above and yellow-green beneath becoming yellow in autumn. Long- or short-pointed, the serrated-edge leaves are sharply double-toothed.

FRUIT The upright fruit is one to one and a half inches long, conelike and elliptic in shape. It ripens in late July and August. Small winged nutlets, one-eighth inch long, are produced in abundance, may average 500,000 to the pound and are spread by the wind.

BARK On the branches and small trunks the bark is silvery gray with a yellow tinge, very smooth and shiny. As the tree grows, the bark breaks and rolls back in thin ribbonlike strips and curls, which remain attached to the tree for some time. On very large trunks the bark becomes rough and fissured into irregular scaly plates, reddish brown to light gray in color.

RED ALDER

(Alnus rubra)
40' to 50' tall — 1' to 2' diameter

LEAVES The toothed leaves of the red alder are generally dark yellow-green on top, lighter underneath and the underleaf may have light rusty hairs. The elliptical leaves are two to four inches wide and three to five inches long.

FLOWERS Soft catkins appear before the leaves each spring. These tassels are three to six inches long. As they mature they shrink into thick cones which are a half to one inch long.

BARK Bark is thin, smooth ash-gray; the ash-gray is often white splotched and mossy. Bark below the surface is a bright red-brown. The smooth bark becomes slightly ridged with age.

Photograph on page 160

EASTERN HOPHORNBEAM

LEAVES The dull yellow-green serrated-edge leaves are lance-head shaped and about three to five inches long.

FRUIT Pendant seed clusters that hang from the branchlets distinguish this tree, these clusters resembling hops, made up of flat, leaflike, seed-bearing pods.

BARK The gray trunk, tinged infrequently with red-brown, is narrowly ridged and sometimes scaly.

FEATURE The wood of this tree is very hard and quite heavy. Woodlot owners of mixed hardwoods are well-acquainted with this tree by its common name, ironwood.

(Ostrya virginiana)
20' to 30' tall — 6" to 15" diameter

AMERICAN BEECH

LEAVES The simple, ovate leaves of the American beech are two and a half to five inches long and have prominent veining running from the mid-rib to the points of the coarsely serrated edges.

FLOWERS Inconspicuous flowers that appear with the leaves in May and early June have stamen and pistil on the same plant, the stamen in globular light green clusters on stems about two inches long, the pistil in two clusters on short, club-shaped white-gray stems a half to three-quarters inch long.

FRUIT The small brown three-sided beech nuts are almost as well known as chestnuts and usually form as a pair in a prickly bur. The kernel is sweet and edible, however small.

BARK The distinctive smooth silver gray to steel gray bark of the American beech is a characteristic which makes the tree easily recognizable.

(Fagus grandifolia)
60' to 100' tall — 2' to 3' diameter

AMERICAN CHESTNUT

(Castanea dentata)
80' to 100' tall — 3' to 4' diameter

LEAVES The leaves of the American chestnut are six to eight inches long, about two wide, and are coarsely toothed along the edges. They are an oblong lanceolate in shape tapering toward the tip and wedge-shaped at the base. From above the leaves are a dull yellow-green and from below they are of a paler hue.

FLOWERS The arched catkins of the American chestnut grow near the ends of the branches in the spring. The flowers are bisexual and grow to about seven inches in length. Eight to twelve distinct furry crowded clusters of flowers grow on each catkin, pale yellow-green in color.

FRUIT The fruit of this tree attains full size of about two inches by mid-August, contained in a spiny, globular husk. This husk contains two or three flat, ovoid shaped nuts. The husk splits open about the time of the first frost and the seeds are very sweet.

BARK The dark brown bark is one to two inches thick. It has a ridged and fissured texture.

WHITE OAK

(Quercus alba)
80' to 100' tall — 3' to 4' diameter

LEAVES Deep lobes on a narrow base distinguish the leaves of the white oak. Seven to nine lobes form a leaf about eight inches long and three inches wide. Gaps between lobes almost reach the center stem.

FRUIT A bumpy textured cap covers the top of the stubby, half-inch-long white-oak acorn. Like the live oak, this acorn matures in one year.

BARK The gray bark of the white oak forms large scales as the tree matures.

LIVE OAK

(Quercus virginiana)
40' to 50' tall — 3' to 4' diameter

LEAVES Thick and leathery oblong leaves are simple in type and green throughout the year. The two- to four-inch-long by one- to two-inch-wide leaves are smooth above and pale green with a silvery white tinge beneath.

FLOWERS The pollen-bearing flowers are light yellow, the stigmas of the pistillate flowers are bright red.

FRUIT A firm, strong stem about an inch to five inches long carries one to five oblong, dark brown acorns each about an inch long in its separate egg-cup-shaped, fuzz-lined base. The acorn matures in one growing season.

BARK The bark on the trunk and large branches is dark brown tinged with red and is furrowed.

Photograph on page 103

NORTHERN RED OAK

LEAVES With usually seven, sometimes nine or eleven lobes, sharply three-pointed at the end of each and each bristle-tipped, leaves are usually five to nine inches long and four to six wide. Channels between the lobes extend halfway or more in toward the prominent center-leaf rib. The dark green summer leaf turns red or red-brown in autumn.

FRUIT The inch-long, half-inch-wide, rounded-end acorns are either paired or grow singly, each from a shallow cup at its base.

BARK The deeply furrowed, ruggedly ridged bark is dark gray or midnight brown in color.

(Quercus rubra)
60' to 70' tall — 2' to 3' diameter

AMERICAN ELM

LEAVES The alternate, simple four- to six-inch-long leaves are generally smooth above and downy below, have double-tooth serrated edges and are asymmetrical at the base. The leaf veins are pronounced and run in parallel lines from the midrib to pointed edge.

FLOWERS The flowers are small, perfect, greenish, on slender stalks about an inch long and appear before the leaves in early spring.

FRUIT The fruit is a light green, oval-shaped samara (winged fruit) with the seed portion in the center and surrounded entirely by a wing which has a conspicuous notch at the end and is hairy on the margin, a mark distinctive of this species.

BARK The bark is dark gray, divided into irregular, flat-topped thick ridges. While it generally is firm, on some old trees it tends to come off in flakes.

(Ulmus americana)
75' to 125' tall — 3' to 6' diameter

HACKBERRY

LEAVES The lance-head-shaped leaf is a distinctive feature of the hackberry. The alternate leaves are green with a dull, hairy surface, deep-set prominent veins and coarsely serrated edges.

FLOWERS Bunches of five thin, dry red-tinged lobes droop, each in a cluster, from a slender stem.

FRUIT A single purple berry hangs from each stem.

BARK One- to one-and-a-half-inch-thick light brown to silvery gray bark is broken into thick scales, sometimes with irregular wartlike ridges.

(Celtis occidentalis)
35' to 80' tall — 2' to 3' diameter

RED MULBERRY

LEAVES The spade-shaped leaves of the red mulberry have coarse teeth along edges, sharply pointed tips and broad rounded base. The young, yellow green leaves mature to a dark blue-green, about four inches long and three inches across. They are more or less smooth on the surface, at maturity, with a slightly hairy texture on the underside. They become bright yellow in the fall.

FLOWERS The flowers form into long spikes and appear about the same time as the leaves unfold. The pistillate flowers are about an inch long and the bright green staminate flowers grow to about two and a half inches. Each spike is made up of many tiny, four-lobed flowers.

FRUIT The long, narrow berry turns from red to dark purple on maturity and is about an inch long. It is sweet, juicy and highly edible.

BARK The thin brown bark forms into irregular plates upon maturity. It has a slight red tinge and is about a half-inch thick.

(Morus rubra)
60' to 70' tall — 2' to 4' diameter

143

TULIP TREE
OR
YELLOW POPLAR

(Liriodendron tulipifera)
80' to 100' tall — 4' to 6' diameter

LEAVES The shiny deep green tulip tree leaves are about five or six inches long and equally wide, with four lobes.

FLOWERS Six chartreuse colored petals form the tuliplike flower of the tulip tree. They are boldly marked around the base with a bright orange margin.

FRUIT The early autumn ripening fruit is about two to three inches long and a half inch thick.

BARK The dark brown bark is deeply grooved on the mature trees, scaly when the tree is younger.

Photograph on page 73

SOUTHERN MAGNOLIA

(Magnolia grandiflora)
25' to 75' tall — 2' to 3' diameter

LEAVES The oblong leaves of the Southern magnolia are not deciduous but remain shiny dark green through the year and are a smooth, wavy edged five to ten inches long and about two or three wide.

FLOWERS The fragrant well-known flowers of the Southern magnolia are white with pink cast, have six to twelve short-lived petals that form a flower up to nine inches in diameter.

FRUIT The singular reddish-brown magnolia fruit is made up of many tiny pods and when ripe, each of the small pods hangs by a threadlike stem from the oblong dense fruit unit.

BARK The bark is usually smooth, sometimes scaly, ashy gray or brown in color. Branchlets are marked conspicuously by large leaf scars, either horizontally or longitudinally.

SASSAFRAS

(Sassafras albidum)
35' to 45' tall — 18" to 24" diameter

LEAVES The leaves are a distinguishing characteristic of the sassafras. The tree is one of only a few on which leaves of both widely different shape and size can be found. Some are single ovals, others may have one lobe, like the thumb of a mitten, others may be divided into three distinct lobes.

FLOWERS The flowers appear in clusters, are greenish yellow and open at the same time as the leaves.

FRUIT The fruit of the sassafras consists of lustrous dark blue or black berries ripening in September and October. They are about one-third-inch globes each on a one- to two-inch stalk.

BARK Deep, irregular fissures separate broad, flat ridges of the dark red-brown bark.

SWEETGUM

(Liquidambar styraciflua)
60' to 120' tall—1-1/2' to 3' diameter

LEAVES The leaves of the sweetgum are probably its most easily recognizable characteristic. They form five- to seven-pointed stars, with the two lowest lobes having flat bases. They are up to seven inches broad, with a serrated edge, and are aromatic. Lustrous green in the summer, they become conspicuously brilliant in their autumnal coloring, ranging from their typical deep red to a pale yellow with shades of orange and bronze between.

FRUIT The fruit of the sweetgum is a thick-petaled globular head, an inch or more in diameter, on a long stem. This head is made up of many seed-carrying capsules, each ending in a projecting spine.

BARK Young trees have ash-gray trunks often covered with a warty, hard growth of bark. On older trees the bark is red-tinged gray-brown in color and is deeply furrowed with the broad ridges broken horizontally, resulting in a scaly appearance.

AMERICAN SYCAMORE

(Platanus occidentalis)
100' to 150' tall — 4' to 11' diameter

LEAVES The leaves are simple, alternate, about four to seven inches long and approximately as wide. They have three more prominent lobes and their palmate structure often shows five or even a small seven lobes. The color is bright green.

FLOWERS The woody flower stalk carries either one or sometimes two dense round clusters of very small flowers.

FRUIT Round one-inch balls of fruit hang from smooth, thin stems, sometimes half a foot long, and are conspicuous greenish burnt orange in winter when the tree is otherwise devoid of foliage. The fruit ball breaks apart in spring, scattering to the wind the small seeds of which it had been composed.

BARK The sycamore can be recognized easily by its bark which is quite smooth and greenish gray on younger trees. As the tree grows, the now brown outer bark flakes off in large patches each year leaving nearly white younger bark exposed. Mature boles thus have a mottled white and brown appearance.

Photograph on page 113

BLACK CHERRY

(Prunus serotina)
50' to 70' tall — 1' to 3' diameter

LEAVES Simple, alternate, oblong leaves with pointed tips have finely serrated edges and are thick and firm. The leaves vary in size between two inches long by an inch wide to six inches in length by one and a half in width. The color is a deep green enhanced by being naturally shiny on top.

FLOWERS When the leaves have unfolded to about half their full growth the flowers begin to blossom. In the Southern half of the country this may be from the end of March to the end of April; in the Northern half, from the end of April to late May. The stalks full of tiny white flowers are attractive — both to humans to look at in the awakening spring and to bees for making honey.

FRUIT The purplish-black fruit, while edible, is about as large as a pea and is bitter.

BARK The bark ranges from a smooth auburn marked by horizontal white lines when young to a characteristic plated dark gray when mature. The tree can be identified easily by these small plates.

HONEY LOCUST

LEAVES The leaves are either pinnate (featherlike) with eighteen to twenty-eight leaflets, or twice-pinnate, consisting of four to seven pairs of pinnae or secondary leaflets, each six to eight inches long. The inch-long leaflets are a shiny dark green above and muted yellow-green underneath.

FLOWERS The honey-rich greenish-yellow flowers appear inconspicuously in June when the leaves are almost full grown.

FRUIT The fruit is a pod often twisted, ten to eighteen inches long and about an inch wide, flat, dark brown or black when ripe and containing hard, yellow seeds.

BARK The bark on old trees is dark gray, divided into thin, tight scales. The honey locust has tough, sharp thorns, both straight and branched; these begin to grow from it after the first year. The sharp spines plus the leaf fronds make the honey locust readily recognizable.

(Gleditsia triacanthos)
60' to 80' tall — 2' to 4' diameter

SUGAR MAPLE

LEAVES The three- or five-lobed simple, opposite leaves are from three to five inches across with softly rounded divisions between lobes, one of the distinguishing characteristics between this hard maple and the soft maples. The leaves are dark green on the upper surface, pale green beneath and in autumn turn brilliant shades of dark red, scarlet, orange or clear yellow.

FLOWERS The flowers are yellowish green on slender stalks with staminate and pistillate on either the same or different trees in same or discrete clusters.

FRUIT The two-winged samara is generally "U" shaped with the broad, thin inch–long wings each carrying a quarter-inch seed near the junction with the stem.

BARK The bark on young trees is light gray or brown and rather smooth but breaks up into long, irregular plates or scales, varying from light gray to almost black, as the tree matures.

(Acer saccharum)
80' to 120' tall — 3' to 4' diameter

Photograph on page 34

SILVER MAPLE

(Acer saccarinum)
90' to 120' tall — 3' to 4' diameter

LEAVES The leaves of the silver maples are six to seven inches long with a somewhat heart-shaped base and five, toothed lobes projecting from the base. The center lobe, itself, may have three smaller lobes on its tip. The smooth surface is bright pale green, while the underside is slightly hairy and a silver-white in color. The leaves turn pale yellow in autumn.

FLOWERS The flowers of the silver maple long precede the leaves in appearance, blossoming in the first warm days of late winter or early spring. The body of the flower consists of five petals with three to seven stamen in the center.

FRUIT Pairs of winged seeds ripen before the leaves appear. The light brown seeds hang from two-inch stems. The wing and seed is about two inches long.

BARK The smooth silver-gray bark of young trees becomes darker and thick upon maturity forming large, thin scales on the trunk.

Photograph on page 93

RED MAPLE

(Acer rubrum)
80' to 120' tall — 3' to 4-1/2' diameter

LEAVES The rounded, broad base of the red maple leaf supports three to five stubby, doubly serrated or toothed lobes. These broad leaves have a smooth, pale green surface while the underside has a white cast with short soft hairs. In the fall the leaves turn a brilliant scarlet in color.

FLOWERS Opening before the leaves appear, in March or April, the flowers are bright scarlet or dull red in color. The flowers grow in long slender-stemmed clusters with five to eight scarlet stamens protruding from the center.

FRUIT Paired, winged seeds droop from four-inch stems. They are dark red in color and about an inch long.

BARK The smooth gray bark of young trees matures into a dark gray ridged bark which forms plates on the trunk.

BOX ELDER

(Acer negundo)
50' to 70' tall — 1-1/2' to 4' diameter

LEAVES The leaves of this true maple — the only one with compound leaves — are generally composed of three separate leaflets but some may appear as three-part single leaves; they are compound and opposite, smooth and lustrous green, on a stem two to three inches long. The leaflets are two to four inches long and an inch or two wide, making the whole leaf about four to seven inches in length.

FRUIT The fruit is a samara, double-winged similar to that of the sugar maple, but smaller. It ripens in late summer or early fall, also like its close relative, the sugar maple, but unlike its other close relatives, the red maple and the silver maple.

BARK On young trees the bark is smooth and green to purple in color, sometimes greenish tan; on older trees it remains thin but is gray to light brown in color and divided in regular furrows.

HORSECHESTNUT

(Aesculus hippocastanum)
(Not Native)
30' to 65' tall — 1' to 2' diameter

LEAVES A cluster of five to nine leaflets makes up the horsechestnut leaf. The leaflets are four to ten inches long and taper from very narrow bases to a maximum of about three inches, two-thirds of the way up, then taper back to a short point.

FLOWERS Showy clusters of cream colored flowers stand upright from the branches, resembling candles on a Christmas tree.

FRUIT A round green capsule with prickles, about an inch to three inches in diameter contains two or more large seeds. These chestnuts are bitter and inedible.

AMERICAN BASSWOOD

LEAVES The leaves are broadly heart-shaped, three to six inches long, two to four inches wide, coarsely serrated, smooth on both sides except for some hairs at the axils of the veins.

FLOWERS The flowers are yellowish white, in drooping clusters that open in early summer. The flower stem is united to the middle of a long narrow leaflike bract. The flowers are very fragrant and bees can make a large amount of choice grade honey from them.

FRUIT The fruit is a dry berrylike, one- or two-seeded and rounded nutlet one-third to one-half inch long, covered with short, thick, brown wool. It remains attached to the leafy bract which later acts as a wing to bear it away on the wind.

BARK The bark is about one inch thick, light brown, deeply furrowed and frequently scaly.

(Tilia americana)
60' to 80' tall — 2' to 4' diameter

SAGUARO

LEAVES The saguaro has no leaves. Tough and fibrous, the gray woody spines one-half to two inches long are located on as many as twenty to thirty vertical ribs around the trunk.

FLOWERS The trumpet-shaped flowers are up to four inches long and about two and a half inches across. The blossom exudes a melonlike fragrance when it opens, nocturnally only, from May to July. The fleshy, thick flower petals are white with a yellow center.

FRUIT The sweet and juicy scarlet fruit which ripens in August is edible and grows to a length of about an inch and a half.

WOOD Lightweight yet strong, the coarse-grained wood is light brown in color, tinged with yellow.

(Cereus giganteus)
50' to 60' tall — 1' to 3' diameter

FLOWERING DOGWOOD

(Cornus florida)   15' to 30' tall — 6" to 12" diameter
LEAVES   Leaves are opposite, ovate, three to five inches long, two to three wide, pointed, bright green above and pale green or grayish beneath.

FLOWERS   The flowers, which unfold from conspicuous round, grayish winter flower buds before the leaves come out, are small green-yellow, arranged in dense heads surrounded by large white or, rarely, pink bracts that look like petals. Together, the appearance is one of large, spreading single flowers two to four inches across.

FRUIT   The fruit is a bright scarlet "berry" half an inch long, containing a hard nutlet containing one or two seeds. Usually several fruits, or "berries," are contained in one head. These make excellent food for birds, squirrels and other small animals.

BARK   The bark is red-brown to black, broken into small four-sided scaly blocks.

Photograph on page 14

WHITE ASH

(Fraxinus americana)   50' to 80' tall — 2' to 3' diameter
LEAVES   The opposite leaves of the white ash are from eight to twelve inches long and have from five to nine plainly stalked, sharp-pointed leaflets, dark green and smooth above, pale green beneath.

FLOWERS   The flowers are two kinds on different trees, the staminate in dense reddish-purple clusters and the pistillate in more open bunches.

FRUIT   The fruit of the white ash is winged, one to one and a half inches long, resembling the blade of a canoe in outline, with the seed at the handle end.

BARK   The bark varies in color from a light gray to gray-brown. The rather narrow ridges are separated with marked regularity by deep, diamond-shaped fissures.

Photograph on page 94

NORTHERN CATALPA

(Catalpa speciosa)
80' to 110' tall — 2' to 4' diameter

LEAVES   The simple, opposite leaves of the catalpa have long stems, are heart-shaped at the base, tapering to a pointed tip and are eight to twelve inches in length, six to eight in width.

FLOWERS   Clusters of white thimble-shaped flowers appear in late May or early June following emergence of leaves. The flowers have yellow and purple markings.

FRUIT   A brown, seedlike bean pod, eight to eighteen inches long, about one-half-inch center diameter, holds numerous one-inch seeds fringed with fine hair.

BARK   The catalpa's bark varies from dark gray to reddish brown and is slightly rough and scaly.

151

VI OF MAN AND THE FOREST

The forest is an ecosystem—an ever changing natural compound of animate and inanimate components. The changes in the ecosystem are produced quietly or catastrophically by the activities of its components.

Man totally, generically, is a social system. The total social system is almost infinite. Within the social system are a myriad inhabitants, dynamic, finite men causing change, quietly or catastrophically within the social system. The ecosystem—the forest, and the social system—man, are much more closely related than is indicated by an "and." They are so intimately entwined and their relationship is so sensitive that each reacts to changes in the other, usually quietly, sometimes catastrophically. Nowhere else in creation is the relationship between an ecosystem and a social system so complex, so beautiful, so rewarding. And so tenuous.

The forest provides goods and services to man, forest products if you will. Forest products include wood for chairs and houses, pulp for paper and many more tangible items. These are a few of the products of only one of the components of the ecosystem. These products appeal to a greater or lesser degree to some of the component members of the social system. Other members have a deep interest in the wildlife product of the forest. Still others are interested in the forest products of camping, grass for cattle, skiing, solitude, pure water, scenery and recreational fishing, and the list continues on and on. Surely the designer of creation approached perfection in the forest ecosystem. For it achieves nearly perfect service to man.

The forest is unique in two ways. It has the capability to provide for most of the needs of man because most of its components can provide several products. Deer provide sport for the photographer, aesthetic pleasure for the hiker and traveler, and sport and sometimes meat for the hunter.

A maturing group of aspen trees in the lakes states intercepts the downpour of rain allowing droplets to reach the soil gently and soak in. When mature, the aspen are harvested and made into paper on which possibly this book is printed. Young aspen sprout in the place of their parents to once again intercept the rainfall, display beautiful fall colors and for the first few years, while they are close to the ground, provide winter food for deer herds, grouse, and if they are close to water, perhaps a beaver.

Travelers in a maple forest stop to enjoy a significant forest product — aesthetic pleasure.

Water, another component of the forest, falls softly from the leaves of tree and bush, soaks into the ground and begins its journey towards the ocean. Enroute it carries nutrients to trees and plants, quenches the thirst of animals and man, becomes habitat for fish, provides white-water canoeing, swimming and pleasure boating. In the valley, it serves man at home, in business, and then through evaporation finds its way back into the atmosphere to once again fall on the forest.

The forest is unique in a second way. Among that group of gifts which we call natural resources, the forest, unlike any other, has the unique capability to renew itself and continue to provide man with the products he needs as the social system changes and new demands are to be met. The great forests of southeastern United States are perhaps the best example of this unique ability. In the early years of our nation, a combination of forest products was

153

Scarred mountainside showing the results of undue carelessness in a logging operation in north central New Mexico.

harvested to support settlement of the country. The forest *renewed itself* and in the middle years of our nation provided a combination of products for development, both industrial and social, which provided our social system with a standard of living previously unknown to man. Once again, a third time, the forest renewed itself and now in modern day United States will produce a different mixture — recreation, solitude, wood, wildlife, and other products that are needed by man today. And, if the past is prologue to the future, then the ecosystem carries with it the promise that it will renew itself again and again, to continue its design for service to man.

The relationship between the forest and man is so intimately entwined that each responds to changes in the other. How unfortunate it is then that men in their finite ability to understand the forest ecosystem, seek to elevate their personally cherished component of the forest above all else to the detriment not only of the ecosystem but the social system as well. *The ecosystem cannot produce only one product, be it recreation, water, wildlife, timber, solitude, or any other of the myriad possible products because either the responsive change in the ecosystem will ultimately severely curtail production of the cherished product, or the social system would not be able to tolerate the disruption of one or more necessary component products of the forest.* The social system, total man, must consider the ecosystem, the total forest, as it moves toward the future. If man seeks a reasonable mix of goods and services the forest will be able to provide them for generations to come.

David B. Lovekin

A fast-sweeping fire left behind these intensely black charred remains.

November 4, 1857. How swift Nature is to repair the damage that man does! When he has cut down a tree and left only a white-topped and bleeding stump, she comes at once to the rescue with her chemistry, and covers it decently with a fresh coat of gray, and in course of time she adds a thick coat of green cup and bright cockscomb lichens, and it becomes an object of new interest to the lover of nature! Suppose it were always to remain a raw stump instead! It becomes a shelf on which this humble vegetation spreads and displays itself, and we forget the death of the larger in the life of the less.

November 8, 1858. Nature has many scenes to exhibit, and constantly draws a curtain over this part or that. She is constantly repainting the landscape and all surfaces, dressing up some scene for our entertainment. Lately we had a leafy wilderness, now bare twigs begin to prevail, and soon she will surprise us with a mantle of snow. Some green she thinks so good for our eyes, like blue, that she never banishes it entirely, but has created evergreens.

Henry David Thoreau
from Journal

On a bed of sandy ground fifteen yards square, which had been occupied by four sugar pines, I counted ninety-four promising seedlings, an instance of Sequoia gaining ground from its neighbors. Here also I noted eighty-six young sequoias from one to fifty feet high on less than half an acre of ground that had been cleared and prepared for their reception by fire. This was a small bay burned into dense chaparral, showing that fire, the great destroyer of tree life, is sometimes followed by conditions favorable for new growths. Suf-

There is hope of a tree, if it be cut down, that it will sprout again, and that the tender branch thereof will not cease.
Job 14:7

Out of death or destruction, out of the stump of a former giant, the forest regenerates.

Cut and sized timber is ready for the pulp mill.

ficient fresh soil, however, is furnished for the constant renewal of the forest by the fall of old trees without the help of any other agent — burrowing animals, fire, flood, landslip, etc. — for the ground is thus turned and stirred as well as cleared, and in every roomy, shady hollow beside the walls of upturned roots many hopeful seedlings spring up.

John Muir
from "The Sequoia"

Any fool can destroy trees. . . . It took more than three thousand years to make some of the trees in these Western woods. . . . Through all the wonderful, eventful centuries since Christ's time — and long before that — God has cared for these trees, saved them from drought, disease, avalanches, and a thousand straining, leveling tempests and floods; but He cannot save them from fools — only Uncle Sam can do that.

John Muir
from *The American Forests*

In the forest between the Middle and East forks of the Kaweah, I met a great fire, and as fire is the master scourge and controller of the distribution of trees, I stopped to watch it and learn what I could of its works and ways with the giants. It came racing up the steep chaparral-covered slopes of the East Fork canon with passionate enthusiasm in a broad cataract of flames, now bending down low to feed on the green bushes, devouring acres of them at a breath, now towering high in the air as if looking abroad to choose a way, then stooping to feed again, the lurid flapping surges and the smoke and terrible rushing and roaring hiding all that is gentle and orderly in the work. But as soon as the deep forest was reached the ungovernable flood became calm like a torrent entering a lake, creeping and spreading beneath the trees where the ground was level or sloped gently, slowly nibbling the cake of compressed needles and scales with flames an inch high, rising here and there to a foot or two on dry twigs and clumps of small bushes and brome grass. Only at considerable intervals were fierce bonfires lighted, where heavy branches broken off by snow had accumulated, or around some venerable giant whose head had been stricken off by lightning.

John Muir
from "The Sequoia"

157

But notwithstanding, all the observed phenomena bearing on the post-glacial history of this colossal tree point to the conclusion that it never was more widely distributed on the Sierra since the close of the glacial epoch; that its present forests are scarcely past prime, if, indeed, they have reached prime; that the post-glacial day of the species is probably not half done; yet, when from a wider outlook the vast antiquity of the genus is considered, and its ancient richness in species and individuals, comparing our Sierra giant and *Sequoia sempervirens* of the coast, the only other living species, with the many fossil species already discovered, and described by Heer and Lesquereux, some of which flourished over large areas around the Arctic Circle, and in Europe and our own territories, during Tertiary and Cretaceous times, — then, indeed, it becomes plain that our two surviving species, restricted to narrow belts within the limits of California, are mere remnants of the genus both as to species and individuals, and that they probably are verging to extinction. But the verge of a period beginning in Cretaceous times may have a breath of tens of thousands of years, not to mention the possible existence of conditions calculated to multiply and reëxtend both species and individuals. No unfavorable change of climate, so far as I can see, no disease, but only fire and the axe and the ravages of flocks and herds threaten the existence of these noblest of God's trees. In Nature's keeping they are safe, but through man's agency destruction is making rapid progress, while in the work of protection only a beginning has been made.

John Muir
from "The Sequoia"

U.S. Forest Service

Cut by a forester, a mature ponderosa falls, its branches and needles swooshing through calm air.

They were felling the dead tree. It was
    necessary.
On the hard ground
Men stamped and clapped for warmth.
Wind, otherwise, hurling against old rot
The winter wind at unresisting rot
Would knock the neighbor beeches headlong
    with it.
The man in red plaid coat secured a cable
The man, blue-hooded, hacked a deeper notch
Men stamped and clapped for warmth and tied
    the noose.
It was all familiar. Cold air, frozen earth,
The patch of woods, familiar, and the crack
Of axe, the buzz of saw; it was necessary.
Hacked branches lay there first. It was a cold
    day.
Men shouted. A woman came and stood.
It was all familiar. There was a splintering
There was a crack and crash. Men leapt and
    laughed, the woman shuddered.

There was an empty hole
Roots stiff as corpses
Sprang out, like arms and legs stiffened in the
    air,
And unfamiliar.

Lenore Marshall
from "Tree"

Who robbed the woods,
The trusting woods?
The unsuspecting trees
Brought out their burrs and mosses.
His fantasy to please.
He scanned their trinkets, curious,
He grasped, he bore away.
What will the solemn hemlock
What will the fir-tree say?

Emily Dickinson

Hurt not . . . the trees.

Revelation 7:30

A fungus-covered spruce trunk graces the forest floor.

Mountain Men

Aldo Leopold, one of the foresighted Forest Service leaders who pioneered the wilderness concept, once expressed his wilderness philosophy when he referred to the early mountain men, such as Jim Bridger and "Kit" Carson, as follows: "No servant brought them meals. . . . No traffic cop whistled them off the hidden rock in the next rapids. No friendly roof kept them dry when they misguessed whether or not to pitch the tent. No guide showed them which camping spots offered a night-long breeze, and which a night-long misery of mosquitoes; which firewood made clear coals, and which would only smoke. The elemental simplicities of wilderness travel were thrills . . . because they represented complete freedom to make mistakes. The wilderness gave . . . those rewards and penalties for wise and foolish acts . . . against which civilization has built a thousand buffers."

Out of his wilderness, out of the freedom of his opportunities, the American fashioned a formula for social regeneration.

Frederick Jackson Turner

159

James Fain

*A wilderness cabin on the North Rim
of Grand Canyon National Park.*

Wilderness

Wilderness is part of the American heritage. This nation was spawned in wilderness, and from the beginning of settlement it has obtained sustenance from the boundless forests on every hand.

Viewed with awe and some misgivings by early settlers of the new world, the American wilderness has been interwoven into the nation's folklore, history, art and literature. Even today, these wide expanses of forested mountains help shape the character of our youth.

The wilderness that witnessed the birth and early growth of this nation no longer spreads from ocean to ocean. But neither has all of it been tamed. Many of these untamed lands, majestic reminders of primeval America, are

*An alder thicket on
Washington's Olympic Peninsula.*

parts of national forests of the United States.

Here, as wild and as free as ever, 9,925,352 acres of wilderness in 60 areas are held in trust by the Forest Service of the U.S. Department of Agriculture for the use, enjoyment and spiritual enrichment of the American people.

In God's wilderness lies the hope of the world — the great fresh, unblighted, unredeemed wilderness. The galling harness of civilization drops off, and the wounds heal ere we are aware.

John Muir

On September 3, 1964, when the President signed into law the bill creating the National Wilderness Preservation System, it assured for our time and for all time to come that 9 million acres of this vast continent would

161

Above: *Range after range of Douglas firs in Oregon.*
Opposite: *Aspen in a mountain meadow.*

remain unchanged except by the forces of nature.

The new law designated fifty-four national forest areas as units of the National Wilderness Preservation System to remain forever natural except for special provisions for certain restricted commercial uses. Included were the 9.1 million acres of wilderness, wild and canoe areas previously established by the Department of Agriculture.

Only in America have such positive measures been taken to preserve wilderness as a national resource. In the new conservation of this century, our concern is with the total environmental relationship between man and the world around him. Its object is not only man's material welfare but the dignity of man himself.

———————————

Within these plantations of God a decorum and sanctity reign, a perennial festival is dressed, and the guest sees not how he should tire of them in a thousand years. In the woods we return to reason and faith.

Ralph Waldo Emerson

For me, and for thousands with similar inclinations, the most important passion of life is the overpowering desire to escape periodically from the clutches of a mechanistic civilization. To us the enjoyment of solitude, complete independence, and the beauty of undefiled panoramas is absolutely essential to happiness.

Bob Marshall

The richest values of wilderness lie not in the days of Daniel Boone, nor even in the present, but rather in the future.

Aldo Leopold

As our civilization grows older and more complex, we need a greater and not a less development of the fundamental frontier virtues.

Theodore Roosevelt

In wildness is the preservation of the world.

Henry David Thoreau

Wilderness Act

Wilderness is both a condition of physical geography and a state of mind which varies from one individual to the next. It is part of the eternal search for truth that involves man's desire to know himself and his Creator.

The Wilderness Act of September 3, 1964, defines Federal wilderness as land ". . . where the earth and its community of life are untrammeled by man . . . retaining its primeval character and influence, without permanent improvements or human habitation . . . (which) generally appears to have been affected primarily by the forces of nature, with the imprint of man's work substantially unnoticeable . . ."

Wilderness Policy

In order to assure that an increasing population, accompanied by expanding settlement and growing mechanization, does not occupy and modify all areas within the United States and its possessions, leaving no lands designated for preservation and protection in their natural condition, it is hereby declared to be the policy of the Congress to secure for the American people of present and future generations the benefits of an enduring resource of wilderness. For this purpose there is hereby established a National Wilderness Preservation System to be composed of federally owned areas designated by Congress as wilderness area, and these shall be administered for the use and enjoyment of the American people in such manner as will leave them unimpaired for future use and enjoyment as wilderness, and so as to provide for the protection of these areas, the preservation of their wilderness character, and for the gathering and dissemination of information regarding their use and enjoyment as wilderness . . .

from the Wilderness Act (Public Law 88-577), passed by the Congress of the United States, September 3, 1964

Land for the Whole People

When the Forest Service was established on February 1, 1905, Secretary of Agriculture James Wilson wrote Gifford Pinchot, first Chief of the Forest Service, to outline policies for the administration of the forest reserves (now national forests):

U.S. Forest Service

In the administration of the forest reserves it must be clearly borne in mind that all land is to be devoted to the most productive use for the permanent good of the whole people and not for the temporary benefit of individuals or companies . . . .

. . . You will see to it that the water, wood, and forage of the reserves are conserved and wisely used . . . .

. . . Where conflicting interests must be reconciled, the question will always

A broad expanse of semi-wilderness in the big Lolo National Forest of western Montana.

be decided from the standpoint of the greatest good of the greatest number in the long run.

Multiple Use

To authorize and direct that the national forests be managed under principles of multiple use and to produce a sustained yield of products and services, and for other purposes.

Be it enacted by the Senate and House of Representatives of the United States of America in Congress assembled, that it is the policy of the Congress that the national forests are established and shall be administered for outdoor recreation, range, timber, watershed, and wildlife and fish purposes. . . .

Sec. 4. As used in this Act, the following terms shall have the following meanings:

(a) "Multiple use" means: The management

of all the various renewable surface resources of the national forests so that they are utilized *in the combination that will best meet the needs of the American people;* making the most judicious use of the land for some or all of these resources or related services over areas large enough to provide sufficient latitude for periodic adjustments in use *to conform to changing needs and conditions;* that some land will be used for less than all of the resources; and harmonious and coordinated management of the various resources, each with the other, without impairment of the productivity of the land, with consideration being given to the relative values of the various resources, and not necessarily the combination of uses that will give the greatest dollar return or the greatest unit output.

Public Law 86-517
86th Congress,
June 12, 1960

Ecology is now teaching us to search in animal populations for analogies to our own problems. By learning how some small part of the biota ticks, we can guess how the whole mechanism ticks. The ability to perceive these deeper meanings, and to appraise them critically, is the woodcraft of the future.

Aldo Leopold
from *A Sand County Almanac*

The Early Forest Ranger

Originally, in 1905, the forest ranger's job was primarily one of protection. Distances and vast areas made it difficult for the ranger to do little more than protect the resources. He used horses and mules for transportation and travel. There were few roads. He rode and hiked long distances across ranger districts larger than some Eastern states. On a $60-a-month salary, he had to provide his own horse. Often the ranger built his own log cabin home which also served as the ranger station. Equipment was limited to a little more than an ax, a string of mules, a saw, his horse and a rifle. Physical stamina and woodsmanship were more important than knowledge of timber, forage, soils or wildlife management.

Conservation is the foresighted utilization, preservation and/or renewal of forests, waters, lands and minerals, for the greatest good of the greatest number for the longest time.

Gifford Pinchot

Idaho's Sawtooth Mountains offer a chance for peace, beauty and solitude.

Orville Andrews

Forest beauty in one of America's most intensively used national parks, Yosemite in California.

It would appear, in short, that the rudimentary grades of outdoor recreation consume their resource-base; the higher grades, at least to a degree, create their own satisfactions with little or no attrition of land or life. It is the expansion of transport without a corresponding growth of perception that threatens us with qualitative bankruptcy of the recreational process. Recreational development is a job not of building roads into lovely country, but of building receptivity into the still unlovely human mind.

Aldo Leopold
from *A Sand County Almanac*

Overleaf: *Old harvest; new water. Tony Grove Lake, Cache National Forest, Utah.*

James Fain

167

No living man will see again the virgin pineries of the Lake States, or the flatwoods of the coastal plain, or the giant hardwoods; of these, samples of a few acres each will have to suffice. But there are still several blocks of maple-hemlock of thousand-acre size; there are similar blocks of Appalachian hardwoods, of southern hardwood swamp, of cypress swamp, and of Adirondack spruce.

Aldo Leopold
from *A Sand County Almanac*

Trees Are Essential

Trees have always been vitally important to America as a nation. They have contributed bountifully to our well-being economically, aesthetically and as a recreation medium. Since colonial days wise men have planted trees in woodlands, backyards and along city streets. When greed began to creep in and threatened to rob future generations of precious forests the people of America started to enact laws to help control this greed.

Trees return an almost infinite number of benefits and services to us and to our lonely interstellar spaceship, Mother Earth. The interaction today between trees and people is, in the broadest sense, symbiotic. They contribute to our well-being and help to keep us alive. In today's hyperactive world we ought to, indeed have to, do the same for them.

Science has been hard at work in an effort to save our trees. Forest *entomologists* are studying the insects that attack and kill trees. Forest *pathologists* are studying tree diseases. The pathologists are also investigating the effects of air pollution on our trees. (Recently the death of many Eastern white pines was traced to lethal concentrations of sulfur dioxide and ozone pollutants.) *Geneticists* are attempting to develop improved strains of trees. *Foresters* are finding methods of increasing the benefits, services and products man derives from trees. *Environmental forestry experts* are studying the relationship of trees within the total urban ecology. In a city, for example, a single tree can mean more than a whole acre of trees in exurbia. We therefore see the need — the *necessity* — of paying special attention to the planting of greenery along highways, streets and in city parks. (It has been estimated that there are about 40 million trees along city streets and another 80 million trees around our homes, city parks and woodlands. As population increases these numbers of trees must increase proportionately and we must learn to care for them in better fashion to assure their health and longevity.)

*A truck trail through
aspens near Durango, Colorado.*

In the Rocky Mountain states, a score of areas in the National Forests, varying in size from a hundred thousand to half a million acres, are withdrawn as wilderness, and closed to roads, hotels, and other inimical uses. In the National Parks the same principle is recognized, but no specific boundaries are delimited. Collectively, these federal areas are the backbone of the wilderness program, but they are not so secure as the paper record might lead one to believe. Local pressures for new tourist roads knock off a chip here and a slab there. There is perennial pressure for extension of roads for forest-fire control, and these, by slow degrees, become public highways. Idle CCC camps presented a widespread temptation to build new and often needless roads. Lumber shortages during the war gave the impetus of military necessity to many road extensions, legitimate and otherwise. At the present moment, ski-tows and ski-hotels are being promoted in many mountain areas, often without regard to their prior designation as wilderness.

Aldo Leopold
from *A Sand County Almanac*

*A spot beneath Pack Box Pass in
Bitterroot National Forest, Montana,
is perfect for solitary fishing.*

Ability to see the cultural value of wilderness boils down, in the last analysis, to a question of intellectual humility. The shallow-minded modern who has lost his rootage in the land assumes that he has already discovered what is important; it is such who prate of empires, political or economic, that will last a thousand years. It is only the scholar who appreciates that all history consists of successive excursions from a single starting-point, to which man returns again and again to organize yet another search for a durable scale of values. It is only the scholar who understands why the raw wilderness gives definition and meaning to the human enterprise.

Aldo Leopold
from *A Sand County Almanac*

Increased Pressures

It is easy to take trees for granted. We tend to think of them as indestructible. We are learning, however, that living things can bear only so much stress before the ecological system goes awry. As stress on man often leads to neuroses, psychoses and many physical disorders, so in a strikingly similar way stress weakens trees and makes them easy victims of the forces of death and decomposition. Scientists have found that some of our trees, which were once thought to be practically indestructible, simply cannot withstand the stresses of today's world. Many of these stresses have been generated by man:

Item — We pollute the air and the soil with chemicals.

Item — We injure the tree roots and wound the stems.

Item — We trample the soil and coat it with cement (without oxygen or water the tree's roots smother and starve).

These, and more, add up to the People Pressure Disease (PPD) which we are hearing more and more about. Backyard trees are most susceptible to this phenomenon since they are situated closest to man. We too often attribute a tree's demise to the work of insects, bacteria, fungi, etc., when in fact it is due to PPD. And this total problem goes unsolved. Current research in this area, hopefully, will alert us to causes, effects and remedies for PPD. Air pollution, of course, is at the top of the list of stress factors for our trees. It has been established that concentrated pollutants in the air can kill or stunt trees. (Many thousands of ponderosa pines died or were injured when air pollution invaded the San Bernardino and San Gabriel mountains in California in recent years.)

As our population increases we need more room for living so we cut wooded lands for home sites. Besides the obvious loss of trees this action alters established water tables.

U.S. Forest Service

Underground sewers and power lines disrupt roots. Driveways and filled areas smother roots; so do walkways and play areas.

The retreat of the wilderness under the barrage of motorized tourists is no local thing; Hudson Bay, Alaska, Mexico, South Africa are giving way, South America and Siberia are next. Drums along the Mohawk are now honks along the rivers of the world. *Homo sapiens* putters no more under his own vine and fig tree; he has poured into his gas tank the stored motivity of countless creatures aspiring through the ages to wiggle their way

Children are eager to learn about conservation and preservation from a parent who will take time to help.

to pastures new. Ant-like he swarms the continents.

This is Outdoor Recreation, Latest Model.

Who now is the recreationist, and what does he seek? A few samples will remind us.

Take a look, first, at any duck marsh. A cordon of parked cars surrounds it. Crouched on each point of its reedy margin is some pillar of society, automatic ready, trigger finger itching to break, if need be, every law of commonwealth or commonweal to kill a duck. That he is already overfed in no way dampens his avidity for gathering his meat from God.

Wandering in the near-by woods is another pillar, hunting rare ferns or new warblers. Because his kind of hunting seldom calls for theft or pillage, he disdains the killer. Yet, like as not, in his youth he was one.

At some near-by resort is still another nature-lover — the kind who writes bad verse on birchbark. Everywhere is the unspecialized motorist whose recreation is mileage, who has run the gamut of the National Parks in one summer, and now is headed for Mexico City and points south.

Aldo Leopold
from *A Sand County Almanac*

Original wilderness home in South Dakota's Black Hills of the conservationist and outdoorsman, President Theodore Roosevelt.

Population Impact

Another impact of increasing population: We seek more recreation area and people take to the hills and forests. We widen our roads to carry the cars that take us there and cut more trees! Those trees that are left along the roadsides often begin to die from stress five to ten years after the roads are completed, partly due to the salt spread on the roads in winter; it washes off into the surrounding area where it affects the soil.

While we as a nation seem to respect and love trees we demand a great deal of them:

- We demand wood products of quality and in great quantity.
- We demand forested recreation sites and watershed areas.
- We demand natural erosion control.
- We demand the natural beauty of green belts around our cities.
- Of course we have to have healthy, green trees in our cities and backyards to help brighten our daily lives and act as natural air conditioners.

If we ask all this we must be willing to give back to our trees more of what they need to exist and give it *now*.

Forest trees are our most valuable, **renewable** *natural resource.*

We cut them and trees grow to replace them. Sometimes we tend to forget just how good a friend to man a tree actually is.

Trees help supply oxygen we need to breathe. Yearly each acre of young trees can produce enough oxygen to keep eighteen people alive!

Teton mountain majesty above Jackson Hole, Wyoming, from Blackrock Lookout.

Wilford L. Miller

Trees keep our air supply fresh by using up carbon dioxide that we exhale and that factories and engines emit.

Trees use their hairy leaf surfaces to trap and filter out ash, dust and pollen particles carried in the air; they dilute gaseous pollutants in the air as they release oxygen.

Trees can be used to indicate air pollution levels of sulfur dioxide, just as canaries were once used to detect dangerous methane gas in coal mines.

Trees provide food for birds and wild animals.

Trees lower air temperatures by enlisting the sun's energy to evaporate water in the leaves.

Trees increase humidity in dry climates by releasing moisture as a by-product of food-making and evaporation.

Trees slow down forceful winds, cut noise pollution by acting as barriers to sound. (Each 100-foot depth of trees can absorb about six to eight decibels of sound intensity.)

Trees give us a constant supply of products — lumber for buildings and tools, cellulose for paper and fiber; as well as nuts, mulches, oils, gums, syrups and fruits.

Trees' leaves, by decaying, replace minerals in the soil and enrich it by creating a humus to support later plant growth.

Trees beautify our world and salve the psyche with pleasing shapes and patterns, fragrant blossoms and seasonal splashes of color.

They deserve our thoughtful care.

. . .Are not these woods
More free from peril than the envious court?
Here feel we but the penalty of Adam,
The season's difference, as the icy fang
And churlish chiding of the winter's wind,
Which, when it bites and blows upon my body,
Even till I shrink with cold, I smile and say
"This is no flattery: these are counselors
That feelingly persuade me what I am."
Sweet are the uses of adversity, . . .
And this our life exempt from public haunt
Finds tongues in trees, books in the running
    brooks,
Sermons in stones and good in every thing.

William Shakespeare

If you wish your children to think deep thoughts, to know the holiest emotions, take them to the woods and hills, and give them the freedom of the meadows; the hills purify those who walk upon them.

Richard Jefferies

The forest, unlike any other natural resource, has the unique capability to renew itself.

The only true development in American recreational resources is the development of the perceptive faculty in Americans.

Aldo Leopold
from *A Sand County Almanac*

Orville Andrews

What could be better? A cabin next to a clear, fast-running stream in tall timber. The scene could be repeated in many American states.

Father and son can enjoy each other's companionship while walking through a wooded city park, enjoying nature's bounty.

177

Richard Wright

A solitary and pleasant sundown hour at the pond, exercising arms, chest, my whole body, by a tough oak sapling thick as my wrist, twelve feet high — pulling and pushing, inspiring the good air. After I wrestle with the tree awhile, I can feel its young sap and virtue welling up out of the ground and tingling through me from crown to toe, like health's wine. Then for addition and variety I launch forth in my vocalism; shout declamatory pieces, sentiments, sorrow, anger, etc., from the stock poets or plays — or inflate my lungs and sing the wild tunes and refrains I heard of the blacks down south, or patriotic songs I learn'd in the army. I make the echoes ring, I tell you! As the twilight fell, in a pause of these ebullitions, an owl somewhere the other side of the creek sounded *too-oo-oo-oo-oo,* soft and pensive (and I fancied a little sarcastic) repeated four or five times. Either to applaud

Autumn sailing in the lee of broadleaf maples and conifers along the Pacific Northwest coast.

the negro songs — or perhaps an ironical comment on the sorrow, anger, or style of the stock poets.

Sept. 5 — I write this, 11 A.M., shelter'd under a dense oak by the bank, where I have taken refuge from a sudden rain. I came down here, (we had sulky drizzles all the morning, but an hour ago a lull,) for the before-mention'd daily and simple exercise I am fond of — to pull on that young hickory sapling out there. . . . I stand on the turf and take these health-pulls moderately and at intervals for nearly an hour, inhaling great draughts of fresh air. Wandering by the creek, I have three or four naturally favorable spots where I rest — besides a chair I lug with me and use for more deliberate occasions. At other spots convenient I have selected, besides the hickory just named, strong and limber boughs of beech or holly, in easy-reaching distance, for my natural gymnasia, for arms, chest, trunk-muscles. I can soon feel the sap and sinew rising through me, like mercury to heat. All the past two summers it has been strengthening and nourishing my sick body and soul, as never before. Thanks, invisible physician, for thy silent delicious medicine, thy day and night, thy waters and thy airs , the banks , the grass, the trees, and e'en the weeds!

Walt Whitman
from *Specimen Days*

The disquieting thing in the modern picture is the trophy-hunter who never grows up, in whom the capacity for isolation, perception, and husbandry is undeveloped, or perhaps lost. He is the motorized ant who swarms the continents before learning to see his own backyard, who consumes but never creates outdoor satisfactions.

Aldo Leopold
from *A Sand County Almanac*

In the woods, too, a man casts off his years, as the snake his slough, and at what period soever of life, is always a child. . . . In the woods, we return to reason and faith. . . . Standing on the bare ground, — my head bathed by the blithe air, and uplifted into infinite space, — all mean egotism vanishes. I become a transparent eye-ball; I am nothing; I see all; the currents of the Universal Being circulate through me; I am part and parcel of God. . . .

Ralph Waldo Emerson

I have loved the feel of grass under my feet, and the sound of the running streams by my side. The hum of the wind in the treetops has always been good music to me, and the face of the fields has often comforted me more than the faces of men.

I am in love with this world; by my constitution I have nestled lovingly in it. It has been home. It has been my point of outlook into the universe. I have not bruised myself against it, nor tried to use it ignobly. . . .

I have climbed its mountains, roamed its forests, sailed its waters, crossed its deserts, felt the sting of its frosts, the oppression of its heats, the drench of its rains, the fury of its winds, and always have beauty and joy waited upon my goings and comings.

John Burroughs

Robert Boyd

Additives join a mash of "digested"
wood chips in the process of making wood
into high quality paper.

Little is to be learned in confused, hurried tourist trips, spending only a poor noisy hour in a branded grove with a guide. You should go looking and listening alone on long walks through the wild forests and groves in all the seasons of the year. In spring the winds are balmy and sweet, blowing up and down over great beds of chaparral and through the woods now rich in softening balsam and rosin and the scent of steaming earth. The sky is mostly sunshine, oftentimes tempered by magnificent clouds, the breath of the sea built up into new mountain ranges, warm during the day, cool at night, good flower-opening weather.

John Muir

When I would recreate myself, I seek the darkest wood, the thickest and most interminable, and to the citizen, most dismal swamp. I enter a swamp as a sacred place — a *sanctum sanctorum*. There is the strength, the marrow of nature. The wild-wood covers the virgin mould — and the same soil is good for men and trees.

Henry David Thoreau

180

March 8. — I write this down in the country again, but in a new spot, seated on a log in the woods, warm, sunny, midday. Have been loafing here deep among the trees, shafts of tall pines, oak, hickory, with a thick undergrowth of laurels and grapevines — the ground cover'd everywhere by debris, dead leaves, breakage, moss — everything solitary, ancient, grim. Paths (such as they are) leading hither and yon — (how made I know not, for nobody seems to come here, nor man nor cattle-kind.) Temperature today about 60, the wind through the pine-tops; I sit and listen to its hoarse sighing above (and to the *stillness*) long and long, varied by aimless rambles in the old roads and paths, and by exercise-pulls at the young saplings, to keep my joints from getting stiff. Blue-birds, robins, meadow-larks begin to appear.

Walt Whitman
from *Specimen Days*

Uses of Wood

Today there are over 200,000,000 people in the United States. We, the public, own collectively some 136 million acres of commercial forestland or two-thirds acre for every man, woman and child in the country. This publicly owned commercial forestland represents about 27 percent of the 500 million acres of forest in America from which salable products are derived. The trees on this total acreage initiate thousands of wood products and contribute most to the net oxygen gain. Millions of Americans use this forest acreage for their recreation.

Some of those same citizens, plus millions of others, use some quarter billion more acres of forestland as parks, wilderness areas or watersheds. These 254 million acres are not suitable for growing commercial timber.

Altogether, according to the American Forest Institute, America still has almost 75 percent as much forestland as existed here when Columbus landed. The total area is about 754 million acres. Surprisingly, perhaps, over 85 percent of private commercial forestland is in the Eastern half of the United States. Most of the nation's wood and wood products come from there — yet this is the same area of the country that has the greatest population density. Also surprising is the fact that those states generally thought of as completely urbanized have substantial forest areas. New York, for example, has 57 percent of its total land area of 30,636 acres in trees. The most heavily forested state in all the U.S. is Maine (90 percent), followed closely by New Hampshire (89 percent). Then come West Vir-

Uses of wood: housing in a conifer forest.

I asked professors who teach the meaning of
  life to tell me what is happiness.
And I went to famous executives who boss the
  work of thousands of men.
They all shook their heads and gave me a
  smile as though I was trying to fool with
  them.
And then one Sunday afternoon I wandered
  out along the Desplaines river
And I saw a crowd of Hungarians under the
  trees with their women and children and a
  keg of beer and an accordion.

Carl Sandburg
from "Happiness"

Skykomish River's north fork (opposite) in Snoqualmie National Forest, Washington. Sheer cliffs (above) rise over a rustic barn in the Monongahela National Forest, West Virginia.

ginia (79 percent), Vermont (74 percent), and Connecticut and Massachusetts, tied at 70 percent each. Of all the states *west* of the Mississippi River, only Arkansas (55 percent), Louisiana (53 percent) and Oregon (51 percent) have more than half of their state's total acreage in forestland. Even New Jersey is above the halfway mark with 51 percent, tieing Oregon. Despite urban growth, the institute indicates that modern forestry has helped keep much of the land green.

While the biggest single owner of commercial forest is the government — state, Federal and county — private individuals, about four million of them, own about 296 million acres or almost 60 percent of the commercial forest. Third in ownership of the commercial forest is the forest products industry with some 67 million acres, about 13 percent.

In this country the people have used the forest and its products on a scale that probably has never been equalled elsewhere. Colonial America began its existence in the forest and, while some food came from the sea or from land cleared of trees, other food for many years continued to come directly from the forest. Forests provided the pioneers with most of their basic necessities even when trees were being cleared as obstacles to agriculture. Today the cornucopia of the American forest lavishes a flow of timber without which our present high standard of living could not possibly be maintained.

The U.S. Forest Products Laboratory in conjunction with the Forest Service has indicated that in a recent year the average Englishman used less than one-third as much wood, in one form or another, as the average American and the American was ahead of the citizen of even timber-rich Russia by more than 50 percent.

The American used wood in all of its tens of hundreds of different forms to the extent of sixty-five cubic feet in a year.

From the early years of our nation up to the time of development of factories during the burgeoning Industrial Revolution, the art of shaping wood lovingly by hand into useful household items was common. The utilitarian was converted into the beautiful with a sense of presence, with time, care, and most certainly with a keen knowledge of the qualities and properties of wood available.

An example of the pioneers' use of wood (above) is a beautifully constructed bucket with holes for fingers in the handles. Wooden benches (below) from an earlier age still serve in the Shaker Meeting House, Poland Spring, Maine.

Maple, cherry, walnut, butternut, poplar, chestnut and pine were some of the woods associated with a myriad items ranging from baskets and buckets, benches and boxes to complex items such as a curly-maple armed rocking chair, a hutch, a cherry plantation desk or a butternut double cupboard-on-a-chest.

Of course products made of wood by early settlers and pioneers were not just for inside the house. The house itself, from its shakes or shingles at the top to its beams, joists and stringers at the bottom — and almost everything in between — usually was made of wood. Even in the brick Georgian mansions of the South interiors were finished in gracefully turned woods brought to elegant luster by hand-rubbing, often with use of natural oils. In those days wood generally was used for fuel, and wood provided several easily extracted chemicals. A few simple pulps for paper were developed from it. Only a century or more later did wood take on more complex forms and uses.

Around the beginning of this century men began to dream of the reality of more sophisticated applications of wood. At St. John's, Oregon, the Portland Manufacturing Company in 1905 experimented with bonding sheets of Douglas fir together and the first plywood was introduced. Modified woods, fiberboards, bleached sulphate pulp and refined chemical cellulose products followed at other places and other times. Since World War II "research and development" became a household term in many fields. Wood and science met in the laboratory to develop thousands of new products that are so commonly accepted today we tend to take them for granted. Years before the war such public and private organizations as the U.S. Forest Products Laboratory (1910) at Madison, the Institute of Paper Chemistry (1929) at Appleton, both in Wisconsin, and the Weyerhauser Timber Company of Tacoma, Washington, and its affiliated companies were all pioneering in important new directions. Starting at the production end of the vertical integration line, the Clemons Tree Farm, owned and operated by Weyerhauser, was dedicated in June 1941, to begin the tree farm movement. In just a decade the acreage of privately owned forestland dedicated to growing and harvesting crop after crop of trees — "Tree Farms" — grew from zero to about seventeen million acres on almost 3,500 farms throughout the country.

The Forest Products Lab (FPL) is the best example of the meeting of wood and science (large scale laboratory) to formulate opportunities for new uses. The focus of its work is the chemist's symbol for cellulose, $C_6 H_{10} O_5$. A tree is about 50 percent cellulose, about 20 to

30 percent lignin (a cementing material between cellulose particles) and the balance consists of extractives and various carbohydrate materials. The FPL is concerned with that chemical symbol (indicative of the complexity of the cellulose molecule) and the several ways in which its carbon, hydrogen and oxygen atoms can be separated and reassembled into useful materials.

The reason for FPL concern is its deep involvement in studies of chemical conversion — the possibility of using the edible sugars from wood as food, of using all the wood-sugar groups to fabricate a wide range of industrial chemicals, and of growing yeasts that might be cultivated as sources of protein, fats and vitamins. FPL alters the little symbol to chain-like proportions to produce plastics that can be spun into textile fibers or molded into an almost limitless variety of plastic articles. All of this is within the laboratory's purpose of developing new and improved uses of wood and wood-based products and to extend the limits of the resource by using all, if possible, of wood residues normally left behind when timber is cut in the forest, sawed at the mill or changed at any step of production.

The normal economic and cultural activities of the United States require enormous amounts of wood-fiber pulp. The average American now uses 566.6 pounds of paper products annually, a total of about 600 million tons. Much of this is used in durable shipping containers, tough bags or packages at the store, or glamorous, colorful shelf packaging. Outside the market place wood pulp is the main raw material for paper — everything from newsprint and magazines to textbooks and books such as this.

This last category — paper — is the focal point of the Institute of Paper Chemistry (IPC). Three chemical pulping processes — sulfite, sulfate and soda — are all intended to accomplish a single purpose: to separate the cellulose fibers in relatively pure form so they can be recombined, either physically to form sheets or boards, or chemically to form plastics or textiles. IPC is interested in the chemical processes as they apply to the development of superior papers. The processes all depend on the dissolving action of chemicals to remove practically all of the constituents of the wood except the cellulose fiber, which remains in a fairly pure state. This is accomplished by "digesting" the wood chips through the action of a sulfite, sulfate or soda under steam pressure. IPC was started in 1929 by two presidents and a board chairman of three different paper companies with contributions of $40,000 from nineteen different companies. Today well over a hundred companies support IPC to the extent of substantially more than a million dollars.

Although the physical products of the forest are legion, there perhaps is none more distinctively American than maple syrup and maple sugar. When white men first came to North America in the early 1600's Indians were seen dropping hot stones in tubs of liquid and later eating the tubs' contents. That first known method of developing maple syrup and sugar was a rudimentary way to evaporate water from maple sap. While the method has changed, the process is identical today. In addition to their exclusively American origin, maple products are distinctive for being among the oldest agricultural commodities and for being crops that must be processed on the farm before they are salable. The sap of only two of the thirteen native maples has high enough sugar content to be used for making syrup and sugar, *Acer saccharum* (called sugar maple, hard maple and rock maple) and *Acer nigrum* (called black sugar maple and hard maple). The former is more common over a wider geographic area and thus more widely used in syrup and in sugar production.

Wood is by far the most important product or crop of the forest, but the forests provide many other products and materials, many of which are harvested annually. Year after year our renewable resource, the forest, can furnish them until, finally, the mature trees that nurtured or produced them are themselves harvested to make way for the next timber crop. Fruits, nuts, berries, mushrooms, Christmas trees, oils, pharmaceuticals, tannins and dyes, turpentine, rosin and even resins, all of these and many more are physical, material products of America's forests, either directly or just one step removed from forest extraction. With the addition of two or more steps the material product inventory of America's great *renewable* resource leaps into the thousands.

Barrett's apprentice, it seems, makes trays of black birch and of red maple, in a dark room under the mill. I was pleased to see this work done here, a wooden tray is so handsome. You could count the circles of growth on the end of the tray, and the dark heart of the tree was seen at each end above, producing a semi-circular ornament. It was a satisfaction to be reminded that we may so easily make our own trenchers as well as fill them. To see the tree reappear on the table, instead of going to the fire or some equally coarse use, is some compensation for having it cut down.

Henry David Thoreau
from Journal

He that planteth a tree is a servant of God. He provideth a kindness for many generations, and faces that he hath not seen shall bless him.

Henry Van Dyke

The trees of the Lord are full of sap.

Psalms — 104:16

When we plant a tree we are doing what we can to make our planet a more wholesome and happier dwelling place for those who come after us, if not for ourselves.

Oliver Wendell Holmes

Indian Masks

Indians of the Pacific Northwest were expert woodcarvers who shaped face masks of cedar as highly conventionalized human and animal forms. The wolf mask (left) and a killer whale on a sun mask (above) were carved from cedar by Kwakiutl Indians who lived primarily in British Columbia. An unusual face mask (opposite), called "Wild Woman of the Woods," was also made by the Kwakiutls.

In the early Iroquois Indian culture masks were carved in living basswood trees. The carver would go into the forest, select a tree, burn tobacco at its base as an offering, and then rough out a mask in the trunk. A notch was cut above and below the mask which was then split from the tree. (The tree did not die.) Now the carver could take the mask home and finish it at his leisure. What he ended up with was often startling and grotesque; distorted features created weird effects such as a long, crooked or hooked nose, stretched mouth, deep facial wrinkles, etc. Horse hair was fastened to the head to simulate human hair. These masks were worn by male members of the False-Face Society at special public ceremonies of which the chief purpose was to cure the sick.

The Haida and Tlingit Indian medicine men had a mask to represent each of their spirit helpers. When they felt rapport with a particular one they would don the mask representing that spirit and perform the cure.

Huge cedar masks, sometimes four feet long, were carved by the Northwest Coast Indians for ceremonial dances which usually took place in their plank houses by firelight. The Indians would don the masks and re-enact legends about ancestors and spirits. The Kwakiutl masks are some of the best examples of this Indian art in North America . . . beautifully carved and painted.

Totem Poles

The Northwest Indians, generally conceded to be the most skillful woodworkers of all the American Indians, in addition to their beautiful masks, carved totem poles of cedar. This is a lost art today but many examples have found their way into museums all over the world. They used symbolic figures: animals, birds, fish, plants or mythical beings which served as emblems or crests of a family clan and often as a reminder of its ancestry. In the strictest sense these figures are not true totems because their purpose is to inspire respect rather than reverence. They are used more like the crests are used in European heraldry. But in the broadest usage they are considered totem poles. There are also house poles, which proclaimed the social standing of a family and were often attached to the front of a house; memorial poles which served as a monument to a departed chief and a mortuary post which was both a memorial and a tomb. This had a cavity at the top which held either the body or ashes of a chieftan.

Generally the totem poles present emblems, illustrate episodes from mythology, and often include some ornamental space-fillers. The myths that are depicted usually concern encounters between Indians and animals and often tell how a certain ancestor of the clan obtained his totem.

It often took six months to a year to make a totem pole and when it was completed the erection of a totem was occasion for a Potlatch — a feast of great rejoicing and giving of lavish presents.

At the entrance to the Milwaukee Public Museum, Wisconsin, stands a red cedar totem pole (left), honoring a chief of the Pacific Northwest Haida Indians. Representative of the often startling and grotesque masks carved in basswood by the Iroquois, this mask (right) was worn in an effort to cure the sick.

Robert S. Miller

Colonial America began its existence in the forest and American people have used forest products on a scale probably never equalled elsewhere. Furniture (above) has always been considered most attractive when made from wood. The textured warmth of wood is also seen in the interior paneling and stairways of American homes (opposite).

The lustrous beauty of wood's rich color is used to infuse an atmosphere of warm comfort into the main living area of a contemporary home.